THE
TRUSTED
ADVISOR

Learn the Hidden
Rules and Win
the Game of
Building Wealth

RICK RAY

Guardian, its subsidiaries, agents, and employees do not give tax or legal advice. You should consult your tax or legal advisor regarding your individual situation.

Rick Ray is a Registered Representative and Financial Advisor of Park Avenue Securities LLC (PAS). Securities products & services and advisory services offered through PAS, member FINRA, SIPC. General Agent, The Guardian Life Insurance Company of America (Guardian), New York, NY. PAS is an indirect, wholly-owned subsidiary of Guardian. Wealth Design Group LLC, Partners4Prosperity, and Matson Money are not affiliates or subsidiaries of PAS or Guardian.

This material contains the current opinions of the author but not necessarily those of Guardian or its subsidiaries and such opinions are subject to change without notice. Opinions, estimates, forecasts, and statements of financial market trends that are based on current market conditions constitute the author's judgment. The information provided here is believed to be reliable but should not be assumed to be accurate or complete. This material discussed is meant for general illustration and/or informational purposes only and it is not to be construed as tax, legal or investment advice. Individual situations can vary, therefore the information should be relied upon only when coordinated with individual professional advice. References to specific securities, asset classes and financial markets are for illustrative purposes only and do not constitute a solicitation, offer, or recommendation to purchase or sell a security. Past performance is not a guarantee of future results. All investments contain risks and may lose value. Index performance returns do not reflect any management fees, transaction costs or expenses. Indexes are unmanaged and one cannot invest directly in an index.

Website addresses noted herein are provided for your convenience in locating related information and services. Guardian, its subsidiaries, agents, and employees expressly disclaim any responsibility for and do not maintain, control, recommend, or endorse third-party sites, organizations, products, or services, and make no representation as to the completeness, suitability, or quality thereof.

GEAR 2014-5679 Exp 8/16

Published by Wealth Design Group, LLC

3040 Post Oak Boulevard, Suite 400
Houston, TX 77056

www.wealthdesigngroup.net

Copyright © 2014 Rick Ray

All rights reserved.

No part of this book may be reproduced, stored in a retrieval system, or transmitted by any means, electronic, mechanical, photocopying, recording, or otherwise, without written permission from the author.

For ordering information or special discounts for bulk purchases, please contact Wealth Design Group, LLC at 3040 Post Oak Boulevard, Suite 400 Houston, TX 77056, (281) 220-2700.

Design and composition by Daniel Ruesch

Cover design by Daniel Ruesch

www.danielruesch.net

Ray, Rick

The Trusted Advisor: Learn the Hidden Rules and Win the Game of Building Wealth

ISBN: 978-0-9907339-0-4

1. Finance, Personal

TABLE OF CONTENTS

9   INTRODUCTION:

Are You Trusting the Right People With Your Money?

Ponzi Schemes Versus Legitimate Companies & Advisors • Financial Institutions Play By Different Rules Than Investors • Many Intermediaries (Advisors) Don't Understand the Rules

19   TRUSTED ADVISOR PRINCIPLE #1:

The Trusted Advisor is Mission-Driven, Not Money-Driven

The Law of Reciprocity • Making a Sale Versus Creating Value • One-Size-Fits-All Planning Versus Comprehensive, Personalized Planning • Trusted Advisors Work For Clients, Not Product Manufacturers • How to Differentiate Between Money-Driven Advisors and Mission-Driven Advisors

32   TRUSTED ADVISOR PRINCIPLE #2:

The Trusted Advisor Understands the Fine Print and Knows What Works in the Real World

The Fallacies of Product Illustrations • The Myth of "Averages" • Your Losses Hurt You More Than Your Gains Help You • The Pitfalls In the Fine Print

46   TRUSTED ADVISOR PRINCIPLE #3:

The Trusted Advisor Actively Manages His Ego

Ego-Self Versus Higher-Self • How Ego-Driven Advisors Harm Clients • How Trusted Advisors Keep Their Ego in Check

59   TRUSTED ADVISOR PRINCIPLE #4:

The Trusted Advisor Understands that People, Not Money, are the Real Asset

Human Life Value • Financial Planning Isn't About Money—It's About Your Hopes, Dreams, & Goals •

Financial Planning Tools Require Context • Control, Liquidity, Use, Equity • Needs-Based Versus Human Life Value Life Insurance Planning • The Myth of "Self-Insurance"

73 TRUSTED ADVISOR PRINCIPLE #5:
The Trusted Advisor is a Coach, Not a Waiter

Waiters Take Orders; Trusted Advisors Make Recommendations • Trusted Advisors Recommend on Math & Science, Not Flawed Illustrations & Hope

80 TRUSTED ADVISOR PRINCIPLE #6:
The Trusted Advisor is a Lifelong Learner

The Value of Designations & Certifications • Trusted Advisors Have an Insatiable Hunger to Learn & Improve • Beware the Know-It-Alls • Three Traditional Investment Myths Exposed • The 10,000-Hour Rule

102 CONCLUSION:
How to Find a Trusted Advisor

108 AFTERWORD:
Lessons On Succeeding Financially From My Summit of Mt. Kilimanjaro

119 **My Invitation to You**

121 APPENDIX:
Belief Statements for Wealth Design Group, LLC

123 ACKNOWLEDGMENTS

125 NOTES

To my loyal clients,
who have trusted me
for twenty-seven years.

INTRODUCTION

ARE YOU TRUSTING THE RIGHT PEOPLE WITH YOUR MONEY?

> "You have to learn the rules of the game. And then you have to play better than anyone else."
> —ALBERT EINSTEIN

IT WAS DECEMBER 2008 as the Russian icebreaker Akademic Ioffe left port on a pleasure cruise to Antarctica. On board was a group of former college roommates who decided a cruise would be a perfect place for a mini class reunion. When his roommate pitched him on the idea, Matt Weinstein's first thought was, "Antarctica is the last place on earth I'd want to vacation to." But as his fellow alumni explained the unique features of the cruise, he eventually decided to join in.

After months of anticipation, the day of departure was upon him and, like all the other passengers, Matt was excited as the ship made way to the eerie frozen continent. He was, by all measures, a very successful person who truly deserved this break from his hectic but highly fulfilling life. He was living the classic American dream. He had followed his passion by building a company doing, of all things, playing.

Matt loved to play. In 1976 he was hired by the city of Philadelphia's bicentennial committee to bring a unique form of interactive entertainment to the city-wide festival celebrating its 200th birthday. Not only did he love being playful, but he also had the ability to create unique forms of play which had never been done before, things like tug-of-war contests using a retrofitted rope with three separate leads at each end so literally hundreds of people could play. He created and led people through dancing games for all age groups to participate in. People absolutely loved it. Matt realized he had a creative knack for innovating new games, which were the perfect blend of silly and fun. More importantly, his games accentuated cooperation over competition, so people had a bonding experience by playing together. Matt's games built community.

The entrepreneur in him saw a business opportunity, and he started a company called Playfair. By 2008 the company was being hired by 350 colleges and universities to help freshman students adjust to their new surroundings and bond through play and dance. Playfair not only helped kids acclimate and make new friends, but it also became a hit at corporate events.

Matt not only played for a living, he also became a top 1 percent earner in the United States. He shared a beautiful home with his wife in the San Francisco Bay area, and meticulously saved until he had a substantial retirement account. He was living the good life. At age fifty-nine, though he was figuratively at the bottom of the world, he literally felt on top of the world.

The trip had been going spectacularly when Matt was summoned to the bridge for a satellite telephone call. He was unalarmed because his speaker's bureau informed him prior to departure they might need to call to confirm a potential speaking engagement. So as he eagerly approached the bridge he thought, "How cool is this? I'm with my old buddies confirming a high-paying gig via satellite phone on my way to Antarctica!"

But instead of the speaker's bureau on the other end, it was his wife, Geneen. "Matt, I just found out Bernie Madoff has been arrested, and we've lost every penny of our retirement fund." He felt sick, like he had just been punched in the stomach.[1]

Bernie Madoff, of course, has become a household name after a federal investigation revealed his investment firm to be running a Ponzi scheme considered to be the largest financial fraud in U.S. history, estimated to have lost $18 billion of investors' money.[2] In 2009 he was sentenced to 150 years in prison, the maximum allowable by law. Unfortunately, while the sentence may be justified, it does nothing to indemnify the losses of his investors.

Described as "charming" and "compassionate," Madoff seemed to be the kind of person you could trust with your life savings. One Wall Street trader noted, "We were all aware his hedge fun had had great returns for twenty years. We knew it was statistically impossible [to have the steady gains for which Madoff became famous]. We always kind of wondered: How the hell does he do it? Every person was curious. But that's where it stopped. You'd stop yourself from wondering. You'd say, 'There couldn't be anything bad.' The Madoffs had such a name—and such an aura."[3]

The Madoff Ponzi scheme is an extreme, though surprisingly common, example of good, hard-working, intelligent people losing money by trusting the wrong person. When Madoff's client list was made public in early 2009, it revealed that some 13,500 individual investors had trusted Madoff and bought into the scheme.[4]

I'm less concerned about money lost to illegitimate Ponzi schemes than I am about the money lost by individuals who do not understand the financial products they purchase from legitimate, well-meaning companies and advisors.

I wrote this book because for twenty-seven years as a financial advisor I've worked with thousands of individuals, and I've witnessed the frustration, agony, and despair of good people who realize their plans haven't turned out like they thought they would. Unfortunately, they simply didn't fully understand the rules of the game.

But the bigger issue here is some of the advisors they trusted didn't understand the rules either. My intention with this book is to empower you to choose the right advisor to help you manage, grow, and protect your hard-earned money. It is to help you avoid the desperate scenario when you realize that after saving for years, you're not going to have the retirement you've dreamed of.

Is this self-serving, given I'm promoting myself as a Trusted Advisor? Sure. But I can confidently do so because I make recommendations based on twenty-seven years of acquired wisdom. One definition of wisdom I really like is "accumulated philosophic or scientific learning," because it accurately describes how I acquired the wisdom to be a Trusted Advisor. And I'm not the only advisor who does so—there are thousands of others who also use my approach. After reading this book you'll be able to recognize them—as well as recognize the advisors you want to avoid.

When you were growing up as a kid, someone taught you how to play the game Tic-Tac-Toe. The first few times you played, you lost because you didn't understand the rules. But the game is not complicated—once you understood the rules, you had a chance to either win or break even every time you played, without exception.

Now you're an adult. You're playing the game of wealth building and wealth distribution. You're doing everything you know how to grow, preserve, and effectively distribute and utilize your hard-earned money. Unfortunately, there are very few people who understand the rules of the game, let alone who are qualified and willing to teach them to you.

In order to play the wealth building and distribution game, you must interact with financial institutions like banks, investment firms, and insurance companies. In order for you to be successful in your interactions with these financial institutions, you must understand how they operate and the rules they play by.

There are two types of financial institutions you can deal with: stock companies and mutual companies. You need to understand how they are structured, because then you'll understand how they operate and, more importantly, who they serve.

The main difference in a mutual company and stock company is whom they work for. Stock companies work for their shareholders and they must provide these shareholders an acceptable return on their investment. An executive team hired by a Board of Directors typically runs stock companies. Mutual companies are owned by their clients/policyholders and are responsible for making money for them. An executive team hired by a Board of Directors also runs mutual companies.

Stock companies have incentives to take risks, as they must focus on maximizing the short-term profits of a company in order to please their shareholders. There is enormous pressure on these companies to meet or exceed the quarterly and annual expectations of Wall Street analysts.

Mutual companies have a different mind-set. They answer to clients/policyholders. Their focus is to guarantee maximum benefits to them, and they are not under pressure to generate short-term profits. The management team of a mutual company focuses on long-term safety, security, and a return for their client/policyholders.

Both stock and mutual companies operate by specific rules. These rules are not inherently bad. In fact, when you use the rules correctly, they can be very positive.

There's no shortage of financial institutions pitching you their latest and greatest products. But not all them reveal all the rules of how their products work—they reveal enough to intrigue you, and in some instance glibly gloss over the fine print, which makes all the difference to your chances of winning the game. They're playing a different game with different rules than you are.

To make it even more complex, the rules financial institutions play by don't come to us from the institutions themselves. Rather, we learn them through intermediaries—representatives, advisors, bankers, etc. These intermediaries aren't bad people. They're not deceitful Madoffs deliberately trying to bilk our money. They're not trying to hurt us. In fact, they believe they're performing a service for us.

The trouble is many of them aren't familiar enough with the rules to use them to our benefit. The banks, insurance companies, and investment firms teach them, the intermediaries, how to promote products and strategies. So many of them only learn surface-level aspects of the products and services they promote. They accept the supposed rules of the game, just as we do. But few of them really dig deep and read and understand the fine print. A small percentage of them really know the rules of the game.

In a nutshell, I believe this is the problem with the financial services industry: Financial institutions set the rules of the game. Then they teach and incentivize their intermediaries to promote their products, and those intermediaries either don't know the rules of the game or are disinclined to reveal to us all the rules. We only get half of the story from people who generally only know half of the story themselves.

We think we're playing Tic-Tac-Toe with the financial institutions when, in fact, we're playing an entirely different game.

The scary part? We usually don't recognize this until it's too late and it can lead to real and drastic consequences. We struggle with getting any kind of meaningful return on our money. We helplessly watch our money get siphoned by taxes, eroded by inflation, vaporized by fees and penalties we weren't even aware of. At retirement age, when we need our money the most, we're shocked to realize the vehicles we'd been saving in religiously for decades aren't what we thought they were. Thus, our retirement years are spent in fear and scarcity, constantly worrying that we'll run out of money prematurely. And finally, we're unable to leave the legacy we've dreamed of because our inheritance gets crushed by fine print we didn't prepare for.

The truth is, all that fine print that can bite us if we're not wary comes down to three primary rules that many financial institutions play by:

1. They want us to give them our money.
2. They want us to contribute it to them on a regular, systematic basis (preferably through automatic withdrawal).
3. Once they have our money, they want to invest it and hold on to it for as long as possible (which explains early withdrawal restrictions).

And the intermediaries who promote the products of the financial institutions play by one simple rule: Do what they believe to be in your best interest based on the information they were taught by the financial institutions.

There is hope. Just like Tic-Tac-Toe, you *can* win the game of building wealth if you simply understand the rules and know how to leverage them to your advantage. Furthermore, your chances of winning don't have to be based on luck or guesswork.

It all starts with having a Trusted Advisor, whose role is to teach you *all* the rules of the game, to read and understand the fine print, and to steer you away from harmful products and strategies. A Trusted Advisor analyzes financial options to see if they will work in the real world.

In this book I'll reveal the six principles of Trusted Advisors so that you can weed through common advisors and identify Trusted Advisors. Just as we can analyze financial products to determine if they'll actually work before you buy them, you can analyze potential advisors to see if they have the right mindset, training, and expertise to work for your benefit rather than their own or for the institutions they represent.

As you read this book, I have two objectives for you: 1) I want you to understand the full story and know all the hidden rules, and 2) I want to empower you to choose the right advisor who can teach you the rules of the game and help you make wiser decisions with your money. Because when you know the rules and have the right advisor in your corner, you can win the game.

TRUSTED ADVISOR PRINCIPLE #1

THE TRUSTED ADVISOR IS MISSION-DRIVEN, NOT MONEY-DRIVEN

"You will get all you want in life if you help enough other people get what they want."
−ZIG ZIGLAR

WHEN I FIRST STARTED WORKING in financial services as a Series 7 licensed investment broker, I was taught to look for the sale when I first met with prospects. I went into every client conversation thinking, "Where's the sale? How can I generate a commission/fee and make money?" After a few years of doing this with mixed results, I visited with my coach and told him I was struggling. He told me my struggle came from being in conflict with my values. In short, although I had been taught to live selflessly and I believed in principle, I was acting selfishly. I wasn't making a living because my prospects could smell my "commission breath" and it created an invisible barrier in my relationships.

My coach taught me the principle of value exchange— value follows value. In other words, we receive value *after* we create value for others. This is also known as the Law of Reciprocity: If we create enough value for other people, we will be taken care of. Thanks to that kind and wise advice from my coach, and by proving the Law of Reciprocity thousands of times, I've learned to shift my mindset from "Where's the sale?" to "How can I add value to these people's lives?"

The intention of common advisors is to make a sale. The Trusted Advisor has the wisdom, experience, and caring which fuels a different intention: to put the client's needs above his own.

But let's be honest here: Like everyone else, financial advisors have to earn a living. And if we don't sell products or charge fees to clients, we don't get paid. There's nothing intrinsically wrong with commissions or fees—they make the exchange between client and advisor mutually profitable and sustainable. It's just a matter of where the primary focus is for the advisor.

Truth be told, one of the primary reasons common advisors focus on "making sales" is a lot of them are not in good financial shape personally—regardless of their production. I've known advisors who were making $1 million per year but who were spending more than they were earning. Advisors who aren't making money, or who aren't good at managing their own money, can be tempted to sell products that help themselves more than clients.

Now, understand that I'm not bashing other advisors. As I said, I used to be that guy who was desperate to make the sale. I learned the hard way. Focusing on the sale, rather than on creating value for clients is fruitless. My point is to simply raise your awareness when you're choosing a financial advisor to help you avoid the kind of advisors that I once was.

Let's examine some of the mistakes made by money-centric advisors.

Hammers and Nails

You've heard the saying, "When all you have is a hammer, everything looks like a nail." It's highly-applicable to common advisors. Many such advisors have access to, or are only incentivized to promote, a few basic products. In this scenario, their job is not to listen to you, analyze your goals and needs, understand where you want to go and then make recommendations that will help you get there. Their job is to simply push the products they have access to—no matter the clients' age, financial situation, or goals.

Let me give you an example of the hammer and nail analogy which I see all of the time. There is an insurance company I'm aware of who is obsessively fixated on the all-too-common "buy term and invest the difference" (BTID) strategy. Their advisors are adamantly opposed to any type of permanent (cash value) life insurance. Their strategy may be appropriate for some people, but they don't understand the benefits and usefulness of permanent life insurance for others. I'm not going to get into the technical details of these competing strategies here; my point is simply the fixation on BTID is another example of advisors carrying around hammers and seeing every problem as nails. For many people and many situations, the strategy is wrong and irresponsible and it simply won't work in the real world. Unfortunately, the advisors who represent these companies are unaware of the damage they are inflicting on their clients until it's too late.

Trusted Advisors, in contrast, have a full set of tools, and they use the appropriate one to solve each individual problem. They understand a twenty-four-year-old single man needs entirely different strategies than the sixty-four-year-old retiring couple. They understand BTID may be useful in one specific situation, but permanent insurance may be far better in another.

I've learned from experience my most important responsibility as a financial advisor is to listen. Before I even consider any products or strategies, I need to understand who my client is. I need to know what their assets are. I need to know where they're exposed to potential dangers. I need to know their hopes and dreams. I need to know what's important to them. I need to know exactly what they want to accomplish.

Then and only then can I offer recommendations, which are designed not to sell what I have and generate a commission or a fee, but to solve the specific problems of each individual client.

I've learned to go into every client or prospect meeting with the intention of adding value in his or her life. Many times this means spending time with them and making recommendations for which I will never be paid. For example, they may need to be referred to another professional, such as a CPA, attorney, or business broker. Sometimes I connect clients with other clients to help their businesses. I start every meeting by asking, "What is it you want to accomplish today?" and then I sit and listen.

My mission, just like other Trusted Advisors, is to help my clients solve their problems and accomplish their goals.

Trusted Advisors Work for Clients, Not Product Manufacturers

Good advertising reps live by a principle, which makes all the difference to the success of their clients: They are not advocates for the business owners who hire them, but rather for their customers. When they climb inside the mental "box" of a business owner, they see things as the business owner sees them. Therefore, they're subject to the exact same blind spots as the business owner. The good advertiser stays outside of his client's box and sees the business as a customer. It is only by being the customer's advocate that the advertiser can speak the customer's language and translate the product features into benefits that appeal to him or her.

A similar principle is applied by Trusted Advisors: They are not advocates for product manufacturers, but rather for the clients who buy the products. They make sure clients have all the facts before they make decisions and buy products.

In contrast, common advisors only tell their clients part of the story. Again, this isn't because they're bad people, and in a lot of cases it's not even because they're after a commission or fee. It's simply because they don't know the full story themselves.

Let me give you an example: I recently had a client tell me he was buying a new house and he had met with a mortgage broker who recommended he purchase the house by using a fifteen-year mortgage. I asked him what questions the mortgage broker asked him to determine a fifteen-year mortgage was the ideal choice for him. His response was what I expected: "Ask questions? He didn't ask many any questions. He just told me I would save lots of interest by using the fifteen-year mortgage."

At the very least the mortgage broker should have asked at least these few questions:

1. What's your effective tax rate?
2. What type of rate of return do you get on your safe investments?

3. Are you interested in exploring your alternatives?

I believe the mortgage broker was really trying to do the right thing for my client. Unfortunately, he didn't ask the right questions and he doesn't seem to understand how to evaluate which mortgage is right for his clients. The reason he doesn't understand is he was making a decision in a vacuum. This is very common in the mortgage business.

I see a lot of bankers and mortgage brokers sell clients on the benefits of fifteen-year mortgages as opposed to thirty-year mortgages, the obvious benefit being the interest savings. One important factor is the tax advantages of carrying a mortgage. In many cases, being able to deduct mortgage interest on your taxes outweighs any interest savings by switching to a shorter-term mortgage.

You also lose control of your money by getting a ten- or fifteen-year mortgage. Suppose you have a 6.5 percent interest rate on a thirty-year mortgage, and a broker talks you into a fifteen-year mortgage with a 4 percent interest rate. Essentially, you've guaranteed yourself a 2.5 percent return on your money. But what if you were to keep your thirty-year mortgage and invest the money that you would have paid into higher payments? In this scenario, you come out ahead if your investment return is anything above 2.5 percent.

Another critical factor ignored by proponents of short-term mortgages is they can actually be quite dangerous because you're locking your cash up in home equity. Suppose you get a $300,000 loan on a fifteen-year mortgage with an interest rate of 4 percent, making your monthly principle and interest payment $2,219.06. You make that payment faithfully for ten years. At the end of that period, your loan balance is $96,388, and let's say your home has appreciated to a value of $400,000. So you're sitting on over $300,000 of equity. But then you get disabled and are unable to work. You start missing some payments. You can't access your equity to make the payments, of course, because you've lost your income and can't refinance. And guess who the bank is more likely to foreclose on: you, with your $300,000+ of equity, or your neighbor who just closed on their loan six months ago and has no equity to speak of? You, of course—never mind the fact you've made your payments on time for ten years. The more equity you have, the more incentive your bank has to foreclose on your home when you can't make payments.

Now let me clarify something: I'm not necessarily advocating that you should never pay off your mortgage. Sometimes it makes sense and sometimes it doesn't. What I do recommend is every homeowner should use some type of analytic tool to determine which mortgage best suits their situation. The software I use makes the decision mathematic, rather than emotional. It reveals the full story and plainly shows all of the financial ramifications, versus simply showing interest savings alone.

My point here is that advisors who work for their clients see a much fuller picture and make different recommendations than intermediaries who represent product manufacturers. Trusted Advisors don't blindly trust what product manufacturers say because they know that manufacturers are operating from their own agenda, which may or may not be the best thing for clients.

Another example of this is product manufacturers and their intermediaries who promote qualified retirement plans, such as 401(k)s, as "tax savings" vehicles. I'd guess that most accountants also teach the same thing. Who has trained them to teach this? Financial institutions and the government. The reality is you can't know if a qualified plan will actually save you taxes until all your funds are distributed.

It's not accurate to call qualified plans tax savings vehicles. They are tax *deferred*, but that doesn't necessarily mean that they save you taxes. While you're accumulating in a qualified plan, you don't pay taxes on dividends, capital gains, or profits. When you do begin drawing on your account during retirement, however, it is taxed as regular income at your current income tax rate.

Therefore, the only way for you to win in a qualified plan is if you take the money out at a lower tax bracket than what you would have paid at the time you deferred it. For example, I recently worked with a young married couple that was in a 15 percent tax bracket. Their CPA urged them to maximize their contributions to the husband's 401(k). While this couple was earning a modest income at the time, their future income will certainly put them in the top 10 percent of all wage earners (the wife was in school to become an MD). If this were to come true and our tax law remain the same, they would pay approximately 39 percent on the 401(k) money when they take it out.

Qualified plans also tend to be more expensive than mutual funds. Furthermore, the government and financial institutions can change the rules on you without your consent. It's even possible they could lock it up and leave you with no control. In the past such plans have carried an "excess penalty" for investors who had more than $1 million in them. What's the likelihood of it, or something worse, coming back? Given our government's history, I'd bet on it.

Product manufacturers—financial institutions— love qualified plans because they give them, the manufacturers, a lot of control and good compensation. And any intermediary who represents a manufacturer will push them because they're told by the manufacturer that they're a tax savings vehicle. You need a Trusted Advisor, who works for *you* and who is focused more on serving you than generating money, to see the truth and learn what's right for you.

One final example: A lot of common advisors believe that term insurance is the cheapest kind of life insurance. But when you analyze it mathematically, taking every factor into consideration, it is actually the most expensive. The best day to have term insurance is the first day. Every day after the first day it becomes progressively worse because the opportunity cost is greater every day.

In the spring of 1993, Arthur L. Williams, a professor of Insurance and Real Estate at Penn State University, performed a study on term life insurance policies. The study included more than 20,000 term policies with an aggregate face amount of $4,000,000,000. It included one to five-year, ten-year, and twenty-year contracts, which contained renewal and/or conversion features. His conclusions revealed what Trusted Advisors have known for decades:

1. More than 90 percent of all policies are terminated or converted. 45 percent of them are terminated or converted in the first year, and 72 percent of them are terminated or converted within the first three years.
2. Less than one policy in ten survives the period for which it was written.
3. After fifteen to twenty years, less than 1 percent of all term policies are still in force.
4. **Only 1 percent of all term insurance results in death claims.**[5]

There are many reasons for this, but the biggest reason is because the premiums get progressively higher as you age. Policyholders drop their policies when they get at or near life expectancy because they can't afford the premiums. They fork out thousands of dollars throughout their lifetimes to never see a benefit from those dollars. This is just one reason of many why permanent insurance is a far better product for many people.

Now, if you've been listening to popular pundits like Suze Orman, I know what you're thinking. Yes, permanent insurance pays higher commissions than term insurance. But there are good reasons for that. You're much more likely to actually derive benefits from permanent policies, both throughout your lifetime from living benefits, as well as your family benefitting from a death benefit. Think of what a sweet gig term insurance is for insurance companies. They collect millions of premium dollars knowing full well that they'll only have to pay a death claim on 1 percent of policies! I don't know about you, but personally I'd much prefer having something to show for the thousands of dollars I've paid for life insurance.

With a Trusted Advisor in your corner, the decision between term or permanent life insurance—or any other financial decision for matter—doesn't have to be emotional, speculative, or based on mere opinion. You don't have to wonder what will happen in either scenario. It's a very simple, logical decision based on hard facts, math, and science, with a clear understanding of what works in the real world.

How to Differentiate Between Money-Driven Advisors and Mission-Driven Advisors

Money-Driven Advisors	Mission-Driven Advisors
Start presentations by pitching products.	Start presentations by asking questions.
Recommend products before fully understanding your situation.	Never make recommendations until they understand your specific situation in depth.
Recommend the same products and strategies to almost every prospect.	Recommend different products and strategies to different prospects.
Use hype and manipulation to sell.	Use wisdom and caring to help.
Sell based on speculative hypotheticals and opinions.	Recommend based on math and science.
Represent and advocate for product manufacturers.	Represent and advocate for clients.

TRUSTED ADVISOR PRINCIPLE #2

THE TRUSTED ADVISOR UNDERSTANDS THE FINE PRINT AND KNOWS WHAT WORKS IN THE REAL WORLD

"The big print giveth, and the fine print taketh away."
–FULTON J. SHEEN

"The individual investor should act consistently as an investor and not as a speculator."
–BEN GRAHAM

EARLY IN MY CAREER I was assigned a few orphaned clients, who had worked with other agents who had left the business. I will forever remember what happened to one of those clients, a fifty-eight-year-old man with a variable universal life (VUL) insurance policy.

Universal life insurance is a permanent life insurance product, meaning it accumulates cash value as you pay premiums and it is intended to stay with you for your entire lifetime, versus term insurance, which insures you for a specified term only (typically ten or twenty years). A VUL offers sub-accounts inside the life insurance umbrella, where your money can be invested in the market. As such, it is subject to market fluctuation, hence the "variable" component.

Advisors have a lot of control as to how these products are illustrated. They have a few variables they can play with, including how much money you contribute and, of course, your rate of return. My client had originally purchased the policy based on a 12 percent consistent annual return, which is absolutely crazy, though it was a common practice at the time.

I analyzed his policy and realized it was going to collapse within two years if he didn't contribute more money to the policy or if the markets didn't perform extremely well. There wouldn't be enough cash value to pay the insurance premiums if he didn't take drastic and immediate action. Unfortunately, I wasn't able to convince him to do anything about it. Sure enough, eighteen months after our meeting, his policy collapsed. The cash value ran out and he was left uninsured—after contributing thousands of dollars into the policy.

Several months later, I reached out to him again and invited him to replace his life insurance coverage. I will never forget the tremble in his voice when he said, "Rick, two weeks ago I was diagnosed with terminal cancer." He passed away six months later. The death benefit of his VUL policy had been $1 million. Of course, his family never received a dime because the collapsed policy didn't pay out. His wife was forced to sell their house and get a job to make ends meet. What happened to this couple is tragic—even more so when you realize it was totally avoidable had they had the right advisor who understood the fine print and used reasonable illustrations.

That's not the only VUL I've seen collapse—far from it. In fact, I've seen very few VUL policies work in the real world like it was illustrated by advisors to sell the policy. Very few advisors really understand the fine print of the policies. Sadly, far too many investors are still buying these policies without truly understanding how they work—or rather how they *don't* work as illustrated. By the way, I know this to be true because I owned one of these policies for almost a decade before I discovered the truth of how they really work.

I learned three critical lessons from working with that client:

1. Never underestimate the value of guaranteed, permanent life insurance.
2. Never buy on illustrations—they mean absolutely nothing. What matters is what works in the real world, not how a product looks on paper with manipulated numbers.
3. When you do look at illustrations, make sure the numbers and assumptions are prudent and

realistic. Illustrating a 12 percent consistent annual return is absolutely nuts.

Obviously, we know we can't depend on consistent 12 percent returns from the market. But let's analyze an even more important reason why this client's VUL illustration was grossly misleading.

To understand it, let's start with the standard process with common advisors: You meet with a financial advisor. She asks you how much money you need to accumulate in order to retire. You give her a number. She does some basic calculations, and then shows you how much money you need to save on a monthly or annual basis for a specified number of years—and at a projected average rate of return. She then prints out an illustration showing you ending up with your magic number at retirement age.

There are so many problems with this standard approach I could write a book about it. (Oh, wait, I *am* writing a book about it!) But for the purposes of this chapter, I want to focus on one specific aspect: the projected average rate of return. I highlight this myth first because most financial products are sold on the basis of rate of return, without investors understanding what it actually means.

As I mentioned, a lot of advisors use this "average rate of return" approach when they are selling investment-related products or developing financial plans. Obviously, if you plug in an 8 percent average rate of return, the final accumulated amount will end up being drastically different than a 10 or 12 percent average rate of return over a twenty or thirty-year period.

The glaring problem with this is two-fold: First, the assumption is completely unknowable. The advisor has no idea what rate of return the investor will receive, and so the entire process is grossly irresponsible for this reason alone. Second, and most importantly, *average rates of return are essentially meaningless for investors.*

Typically, if the illustration is based on, say, a 10 percent average rate of return, it will show the investor receiving a steady 10 percent return every year. But remember, financial markets are not constant. Your returns will fluctuate based on market performance.

In essence, any illustration that shows you getting the same positive return year in and year out is a blatant lie. When you base product illustrations on actual market performance history, it drastically changes the end result. The least financial advisors can do is based their illustrations and projections on reality.

> *"Torture numbers and they will confess to anything."* –Gregg Easterbrook

But it gets even more complex than this. Actually showing a market fluctuation-based illustration is just one part of the equation. But when you actually do that, the average rate of return becomes meaningless—it doesn't accurately reflect what you the investor will actually end up with.

Here's a really simple example to demonstrate: Suppose I invest $10,000 in a variable account, like a mutual fund. The first year I enjoy a 100 percent rate of return. Sweet! My account balance is now at $20,000. But the next year my account drops by 50 percent. Bummer—I'm now back to my original $10,000. In year three, the market rebounds and my account gets a 100 percent rate of return, so I'm back up to $20,000. Year four drops 50 percent again, so I'm down to my original $10,000.

In this example, what is the average rate of return of my account? 25 percent (100 − 50 + 100 − 50 ÷ 4 years = 25). But what is my *actual* rate of return? 0 percent. (And note that I'm not even accounting for management fees and inflation, so in actuality this would be a loss for me.)

$10,000 Placed in a Mutual Fund for 4 Years		
Year	% Return	$ Return
1	+100	$20,000
2	-50	$10,000
3	+100	$20,000
4	-50	$10,000
Average Return: +25% Actual Yield: 0%		

This is a hypothetical example and is not intended to represent the performance of any particular product or security.

Consider another example in which I place $100,000 in a mutual fund. My first year my account drops by 50 percent, so I'm down to $50,000. The next year my account rises by 50 percent, so my $50,000 grows to $75,000. The average rate of return is 0 percent, even though my actual return is -25 percent.

Both of these very simple illustrations demonstrate a critical truth in financial planning: **Your losses hurt you much more than your gains help you.** If you lose 50 percent of an investment, to get back to your original amount you need to get a *100* percent rate of return—not the 50 percent that most people would say. The more capital you lose, the less you can benefit from market gains.

I bring up this point for a couple reasons. First, I want to underscore the absurdity of financial advisors selling products based on average rates of return. Don't ever let any advisor get away with that—it's all bunk. What matters is your actual rate of return, and that is hugely impacted by market fluctuations.

Second, when you understand this point, you begin to realize the value of certainty with your investments. One of my responsibilities is to help shield my clients from unnecessary market fluctuations. A steady 3 percent rate of return for four years is a better outcome than the four-year scenario I outlined above.

Don't get me wrong—preservation of capital is not our singular goal (and I aim for much higher returns than with my clients). Still, when you understand just how badly losses hurt your long-term prospects, you assess risk differently, and you place a higher value on safety of principal.

Okay, so maybe you're thinking my examples aren't useful because the numbers aren't true to life. I just wanted to make it simple to illustrate the point, but let's make this more real for you.

On FoxBusiness.com, financial advisor Erik Krom gives the example of the Dow Jones since 1930. "If you add up every number and divide it by 81 years," he writes, "the return 'averages' 6.31 percent; however, if you do the math like we did above, you get an 'actual' return of 4.31 percent. Why is this so important? If you invested $1,000 back in 1930 at 6.31 percent you would have $142,000 [in 2012], at 4.31 percent you would only have $30,000. The impact of evaluating average returns as the only measurement could be devastating."[6]

Rate of return is perhaps the greatest motivating factor for most investment decisions. Yet it is astounding how few people actually understand how it works and what it means to the growth (or stagnation) of our money. Most people use average rate of return to evaluate the performance of investments, when in fact it is profoundly misleading.

> **Myth:** Average returns are an accurate indicator of investment performance.

PRINCIPLE #2   39

> **Trusted Advisor Rule:** Average returns are meaningless. What matters is your actual return, which is impacted by market fluctuations, fees, taxes, and inflation. Never, ever let any advisor sell you on any financial product by touting the average rate of return.

I can't count the number of clients I've worked with who were told by common advisors that they were all set for retirement based on linear math—in other words, illustrations showing consistent annual returns. But then they had to go to work because of drops in the market, which weren't accounted for in their illustrations. (This is why it's essential to have your basic retirement expenses covered with a stable income source which can't fluctuate with the market, which we'll discuss later.)

Here's the point: With any financial product, there are illustrations and there's what actually works in the real world. And what works in the real world is profoundly impacted by the fine print, which most advisors, let alone investors, don't even begin to understand.

One example of this is the fine print is found in sales literature of Equity-Indexed Universal Life Insurance (EIUL) policies.

> **Equity-Indexed Universal Life:** A permanent life insurance policy that allows policyholders to tie accumulation values to a stock market index. Indexed universal life insurance policies typically contain a minimum guaranteed fixed interest rate component along with the indexed account option. Indexed policies give policyholders the security of fixed universal life insurance with the growth potential of a variable policy linked to indexed returns. –Source: Investopedia

These are hot products right now because, as they're promoted, they give you all the upside of the market but none of the downside. Unfortunately, there is definitely a downside to these products. The fine print of most EIUL products states that the company has the right to change the participation rate and cap at their discretion.

The participation rate "determines how much of the index's gain will be used to calculate the interest rate that is applied to your cash value. If the participation rate is 100 percent, then all of the gain in the equity index will be credited as interest to your cash value, subject to a cap. The cap is the maximum percentage of interest that will be applied to your cash value during any indexing period."[7]

Facts You Should Know about Equity-Indexed Universal Life Insurance

- The Cap Rate is the maximum percentage credit a client can receive in an index segment.

- Cap Rates have been trending downward over the last few years.

- The average is currently between 10-11 percent.

- The Floor Rate is usually 0 percent. Some companies offer a 1-3 percent floor, which is usually accompanied by a lower Cap Rate.

- Even if a client receives a 0 percent credit, insurance charges still apply, meaning a client can have a negative return on their cash value during market downturns.

- Cap Rates can be changed at the company's discretion subject to the guaranteed minimum stated in the contract (usually 3-4 percent).

- EIUL is a fixed product—no separate accounts, no actual ownership of any equities. Company strength is important.

- Net Premiums are deposited into the company's general account.

Let me ask you this: Would you ever sign a financial contract in which you are obligated by the contract but the other party to the contract can change its part of the deal? I've never had a client answer "yes" to this question—but that's exactly what you're doing when you buy an EIUL in which the company can change the participation rate and cap, which is very common.

Company	Product	Cap Rate: Jan 2008	Cap Rate: June 2013	Net Change	Number of Changes	Guaranteed Cap Rate
American General	Elite Index UL	11.00%	10.00%	-1.00%	8	0.00%
Axa Equitable	Athena IUL	12.00%	12.00%	0.00%	3	3.00%
Aviva	Lifetime Builder III	12.00%	11.50%	-0.25%	3	4.00%
Columbus Life	Indexed Explorer Plus	11.50%	12.00%	0.50%	17	3.00%
Life of the Southwest	Secure Plus Provider	12.50%	10.50%	-2.00%	3	3.10%
Minnesota Life	Eclipse IUL	17.00%	13.00%	-4.00%	4	0.00%
Pacific Life	Pacific Indexed Accumulator 4	13.00%	12.00%	-1.00%	1	3.00%
Penn Mutual	Accumulation Builder II	14.00%	12.00%	-2.00%	2	4.00%

Source: Company Publications. Since Cap Rates can change at company discretion, information is believed to be accurate as of October 2013.

Another example of potentially harmful fine print is found in group disability insurance policies. I've worked with hundreds of clients who had worked with other stockbrokers and/or financial planners who had never pointed out the flaws in their disability insurance policies. The key to any disability policy is how the insurance company defines "total disability." For example, here's the definition inside a good policy: "You are disabled if due to injury or sickness you are not able to perform the material and substantial duties of your occupation, even if you are gainfully employed in another occupation."

However, most employer-sponsored group long-term disability insurance policies don't consider you disabled if you can do "any job." Here's the typical definition of "disability" in these dangerous plans: "Because of sickness or injury you are unable to perform the material and substantial duties or your occupation, **or any occupation for which you are deemed reasonably qualified by education, training, or experience**." This definition essentially leaves the determination of whether or not you are disabled up to the insurance company. For example, a heart surgeon with a policy like this who loses his hand may not be covered if the insurance company determines that he can work as a teacher. I've worked with a lot of clients who had policies with this definition and thought that they were totally covered.

A lot of people think group disability insurance is good because it's cheap. But, as with anything, you get what you pay for. It's conceivable that a highly-paid professional would not receive disability benefits if they could flip hamburgers at McDonald's after an injury prevents them from working in their chosen field. Many people who simply shop for the best disability insurance rate end up with this type of coverage. A disability policy with such a broad definition of disability defeats the whole purpose of having the policy in the first place. The point of disability insurance is to cover any loss of income if you're unable to do the material and substantial duties of your particular occupation.

If your advisor isn't reading the fine print, he or she doesn't know what will work in the real world. You could be forking out a lot of cash for insurance policies, which won't even cover you when you need them because of strategic exceptions hidden within the fine print. You may have purchased dangerous and/or poor-performing products based on ridiculous hypothetical illustrations that don't accurately reflect what happens in the real world.

The Trusted Advisor reads and understands the fine print. He warns you when you're being hoodwinked because you don't have all the information. He bases his recommendations on what works in the real world, not hypotheticals which look good on paper. And he does this because he's focused on serving your needs.

TRUSTED ADVISOR PRINCIPLE #3

THE TRUSTED ADVISOR ACTIVELY MANAGES HIS EGO

"Ego stops you from getting things done and getting people to work with you. That's why I firmly believe that ego and success are not compatible."
—HARVEY MACKAY

Let me start this chapter by giving you my definition of "ego," which I learned from my mentor, Steve Annunzio (www.SoulPurposeInstitute.com). I define ego as "easing God out."

All right, I can see you rolling your eyes and hear your thoughts now: *Really? We're going to talk about God in a financial book?*

Yep, we are. I want to make sure when I refer to God in this context I am referring to "higher self" in every human being.

But I just want to know how to make more money. I want to see numbers and proof.

Trust me—this has direct implications for your wealth. Stick with me and I'll show you how this is going to help you—a *lot*.

First let me say that I'm not trying to impose any conception of "higher self" onto you. I'm using "higher self" in the most universal sense possible. And what I'm really referring to is something that I believe is inside of all of us.

I believe that human nature is comprised of two sides: our ego-self and our higher-self. The ego-self is our dark side. It's the source of all selfishness, pride, fear, greed, deception, jealousy, rage, lust, pettiness—all the junk every religion and spiritual tradition in the world tries to get us to overcome. The ego-self believes we live in a zero-sum, win-lose world where every dollar you make takes a dollar from someone else. It tries to get you to believe the world revolves around you and your needs. It is naturally a hoarder—it wants you to hoard your money and other material resources, your knowledge, your skills, your talents, and keep everything for yourself. The ego is a victim. It refuses to accept responsibility for anything and is constantly trying to place blame on others. The ego would have you believe nothing is your fault and every time you're in a bad spot someone else has victimized you.

My mentor, Steve D'Annunzio, explains that the ego-thinking mind thrives in six key ways:

1. **Rehashing the Past:** Continually overlaying prior

negative events onto the moment of now, which limits present joy and growth.
2. **Future Fantasies:** Dreaming and worrying about the future without focusing on the reality of the present, which causes paralysis.
3. **Projections:** Superimposing one's personal experiences, thoughts, and meanings onto others and erroneously believing they are truth, which causes mental and spiritual blindness.
4. **Return of the Victim:** Repetition of a past moment of helplessness and/or wallowing in it for the perverse inner "juice" derived from playing the victim, which causes disempowerment.
5. **Random Repetitions:** A mind loop in which the ego obsessively replays a thought or event, which causes confusion and clutter.
6. **Polarized Opinions:** Perceiving a conversation or idea, which ignites an automatic positionality, or side taken against another side, which causes vehement frustration, negativity, or even violence.

In contrast, our higher-self is our purest, highest, spiritual self beneath the mental realm of the ego-thinking mind. Whereas the ego-self fabricates its own version of reality, the higher-self is a sincere seeker of absolute truth. The ego-self is about making up beliefs to serve its own vile purposes, the higher-self is about aligning with and submitting to true principles. It is operating from the higher-self that we find love, kindness, caring, humility, confidence, and peace. Whenever you feel prompted to serve others, that's your higher-self in action. The higher-self understands that the nature of the universe is abundance, and therefore seeks win-win relationships. It is concerned not with meeting our selfish needs, but serving the greater good for all. It is naturally a sharer of light, love, and resources.

Higher-Self	Ego-Self
Love	Fear
Confidence	Worry
Faith	Doubt
Learning	Blaming
Serving	Prideful
Humble	Narcissistic
Asking	Demanding
Empowering	Controlling
Thy Way	My Way

I'm not going to get into all the spiritual disciplines for overcoming the ego-self and accessing the higher-self. My point here is to simply establish these two sides of human nature exist in all of us, by whatever name you want to call them. I think you know what I'm talking about. You've had times, just as I've had, where you've done selfish and stupid things you regretted, which you felt compelled to do by some force inside of you. And you've also had times when you've been kind and generous, prompted by a light within you.

This is all great, Rick, but what in the world does it have to do with my money? Good question. The answer is that it has *everything* to do with your money.

Does the name Allen Stanford ring a bell? He was the founder and chairman of the Stanford Financial Group of Companies that was headquartered in Houston, Texas. In early 2009 Stanford's company was investigated by the Securities and Exchange Commission (SEC) and was found to be operating a massive Ponzi scheme, which bilked investors of some $7 billion over twenty years. He's currently serving a 110-year Federal prison sentence in Sumter County, Florida. What makes a man so greedy and deceptive? The ego-self. And what makes people believe the speculative claims and pursue the high returns promised by such charlatans? The ego-self.

Bernie Madoff and Allen Stanford are both extreme examples of the ego-self in action. But the ego-self constantly rears its ugly head in other, subtler forms in financial planning—with both advisors and clients.

Ego-driven advisors don't really care about clients; they care about money. They can be charismatic salesmen and "hard closers" who are constantly pushing prospects to close the deal. They'll say and do almost anything to convince prospects to buy—including showing speculative, unsustainable numbers on product illustrations. They are so blinded by short-term greed they fail to build long-term relationships. In some cases, they'll actually break laws. In most cases they technically stay within legal bounds, but make poor and even unethical recommendations.

The simplest and most common manifestation of advisors being ego-driven is promoting products, which are easy to sell, rather than taking the time to do the hard and right things. For example:

- It's easier to sell term life insurance than it is to sell permanent insurance, even though in many cases permanent insurance is far better for clients. But term insurance is a faster sell, and therefore pays advisors faster.

- It's easier to sell investments that make clients money, rather than dealing with insurance that protects clients. I can't tell you how often I've worked with clients whose previous advisor(s) left them exposed to incredible amounts of risk because they focused solely on selling them investments.

- It's easier to sell products that illustrate well but don't actually work in the real world than it is to sell less "sexy" but more dependable products.

- It's easy to sell "cutting-edge" products that appear to have tax advantages, which may or may not be true. Examples include charitable split dollar plans, investment-owned life insurance, Section 419 plans, some 412(i) plans, etc. All too often advisors sell seductive products like these without really understanding the fine print, which makes them far less appealing.

- It's easy to give clients what they think they want, rather than what they actually need. For example, suppose a young married couple tells me they want to talk about college planning for their children. It would be very easy to show them the alternatives to plan for their children's education, which would more than likely generate an investment client. But this would be malpractice if I didn't first ask to review their life and disability protection. There is an order in which financial planning should be done (protection first, investments second) and I would be compromising my values if I didn't bring up the protection component before selling them an investment.

- One of the most troubling things I see in the business is advisors who are willing to believe anything just because one person or company believes it to be legal. I can't tell you how many times I have seen speculative schemes crash and burn.

In short, the ego manifests itself in advisors any time they put their desire to sell products over their duty to serve their clients.

The ego-self also manifests in clients. It puts dollar signs in their eyes and makes their heart race when they're presented with speculative deals promising fantastically high returns. It makes them fearful and suspicious, which in turn leads to them hoarding their cash in bad products, such as CDs. It makes them believe money is the asset, not people, thus leading them to become selfish and prideful.

Lest you think I'm pointing fingers, please understand I'm not immune to the effects of my ego-self, either. I'll admit it, like many advisors, during my first few years in the business I allowed my ego to get in the way by rushing my process so I could get paid faster. Typically, the steps I take prospective clients through are as follows:

1. **Get to know the client on a personal level.** This allows me to understand what's important to the client. Financial success means different things to different people and it's wrong for me to impose my personal beliefs on a client. (For instance, I was taught to tithe but many of my clients were not taught the same thing so it would be wrong for me to allow my personal beliefs to influence how I deal with my clients in this area.)
2. **Determine what the client is doing right and wrong.** Almost every client I work with is doing some things right, and also has some blind spots they need to address and remedy. The analogy I use with clients is to tell them to think of a bucket that you're trying to fill up with water. The bucket has holes in it. To fill up the bucket faster, would you rather turn up the flow of water (increase your income and/or

investment contributions) or take some time to patch the holes (address the blind spots in your financial plan where you're leaking cash)? Most clients say it would be wiser to patch the holes first, and I agree. However, most advisors are more concerned with the flow (how much money is going in).

3. **Make recommendations to "patch the holes in their bucket."** Once I see the problems, I show my client how to make their financial plan perform more efficiently.

4. **Make recommendations to enhance what a client is doing.** Once I have helped a client "patch the holes," then I show them how to enhance their plan.

Sounds simple and wise, right? Well, in my early days, I allowed my ego to get in the way in several ways throughout that process, including the following:

1. I spent way too little time getting to know my clients on a personal level; I was trying to hurry the process up in order to generate some revenue. I spent most of my first meeting with them talking about me, my process, my expertise, the company I work for, etc. I probably talked about 90 percent of the time and the client talked about 10 percent of the time. Once I got my ego under control, I started spending 80 percent of my time listening and 20 percent talking.

2. As soon as I saw a way to enhance their situation I would immediately go for it. For example, if a client had money in taxable CDs, I would

immediately recommend a fixed annuity to reduce their taxes. In some cases, I would later find out that the client was in a very low tax bracket so the annuity did them very little good.

3. I would go directly to investments and bypass protection (insurance and estate planning) because investment revenue is immediate, versus protection components, which require time for underwriting and in many cases don't generate a commission to me (property and casualty insurance, for example).

4. I would lead with a product instead of planning. Before getting into this business I was a teacher and coach. So at the beginning I would meet with teachers and sell them 403(b) Tax Sheltered Annuity plans instead of trying to get them to do comprehensive planning. Once again, it was quicker.

Using the spiritual disciplines taught to me by Steve D'Annunzio and other mentors in my life, such as prayer, meditation, active forgiveness, and non-attachment, I've learned to keep my ego in check. However, it doesn't mean I'm completely free of ego or I'll ever be. But it does mean I'm conscious of the effects of the ego and its desire to get me to "edge God out," or in other words to act in inappropriate ways. Operating from the higher-self, or "keeping

God in," helps me to do the right things for clients regardless of the consequences.

Warren Buffet has a famous saying, which is his core advice to investors: "Be fearful when others are greedy, and greedy when others are fearful." Now, I understand what he's driving at, but the truth is that fear and greed are simply two sides of the same coin called the ego-self. I'd rather my clients be wise and peaceful no matter what markets are doing, no matter what other people do. In short, I'd rather my recommendations and my clients' financial decisions be based on higher-self thinking rather than ego-self thinking.

One technique I use to ensure that my recommendations are not ego-driven is to imagine each one of my clients is a member of my family; I would never dream of misleading a family member. I also hold myself accountable to my management team. I review my ideas and recommendations with them to make sure I am not acting selfishly.

Trusted Advisors are aware of the ongoing battle between the ego-self and the higher-self. They're conscious of the temptation to make quick sales by giving inferior recommendations. They operate according to principles, which they are not willing to violate regardless of whether it helps them personally or not. (For example, I know I could make a fortune selling indexed universal life, but I don't believe it will work in the real world so I refuse to sell it.)

Trusted Advisors understand the karmic principle which givers receive. They serve first, having confidence they will receive benefits for doing so. They always seek to create win-win relationships.

Another critical point: Trusted Advisors have no problem saying "I don't know" and are willing to ask for help. Far too many advisors are so concerned about appearing as the end-all, be-all expert that they fake their way through things they don't understand.

It's really easy to develop hubris in this business, especially after doing it for twenty-seven years as I have. But if there's anything I've learned, it's I can never learn everything there is to know about financial planning. For example, I once worked with a client who needed to use life insurance within his qualified plan. I didn't know the first thing about this strategy, but I have a friend who's an expert on the subject. I called him up and we worked with the client together and helped the client accomplish what she wanted. Everyone benefitted because I was willing to say "I don't know, let me find out."

Of all the enemies to your wealth—taxes, inflation, changing laws, etc.—*nothing* is more insidious and destructive than ego. Making ego-based decisions yourself, and following ego-based recommendations from advisors will do far more to erode your wealth than any other factor. To protect and grow your wealth, you need a Trusted Advisor who actively manages his or her ego.

TRUSTED ADVISOR PRINCIPLE #4

THE TRUSTED ADVISOR UNDERSTANDS THAT PEOPLE, NOT MONEY, ARE THE REAL ASSET

"They who are of the opinion that money will do everything, may very well be suspected to do everything for money."
–GEORGE SAVILE

"Money is nothing but a representation of the real elements of productivity: applied human creativity and knowledge. Money isn't the root or primary cause of anything—it is an inert, inanimate object. It is not an actor; it is acted upon."
–GARRETT GUNDERSON
in Killing Sacred Cows: Overcoming the Financial Myths that are Destroying Your Prosperity

H E STOOD AT THE PODIUM in front of a class full of college students, a mature senior with white flat-topped hair and horn-rimmed glasses in a conservative dark suit. It was clear that he was used to lecturing; his voice was crisp and authoritative, his pace deliberate to allow every word to sink in. "Character is really the pedestal upon which everything else is based," he sermonized. "If you want to crush your whole existence, just blacken your character and you'll never hear the last of it. Always remember this, no matter how many good things you do."[8]

The sign beside him read, in all caps:

SIX BASIC FACTORS UNDERLYING the HUMAN LIFE VALUE:

1. CHARACTER
2. PRODUCTIVITY
3. GOOD HEALTH
4. INVESTMENT IN EDUCATION
5. CREATIVE ABILITY
6. PERSISTENCY

The man at the lecture podium was Dr. Solomon Huebner, known as the "father of insurance education" and the originator of the concept of "human life value," as applied to life insurance, in the early 1900s. His classic work, *The Economics of Life Insurance*, has become a standard in the industry.

"Each human life potentially has an economic value," Huebner taught, "which is derived from its earning capacity and the financial dependency of other lives on that earning capacity." His formula for calculating one's human life value is the present capitalized value of a person's net future earnings after subtracting self-maintenance costs, income taxes and life insurance premiums being paid.

But whatever the financial calculations and considerations, Huebner's contribution is to focus on the value of human beings, rather than dollars, as evidenced by the six factors listed above he said underlie the concept of human life value.

Trusted Advisors, like Huebner, focus on their clients, not just the money. They understand underlying a couple's savings is their dreams to give their children a great education. Underlying annuity payments are grandparents' desires to visit their grandchildren. Underlying life insurance premiums is all the person holds dear, which is far more important than money.

Trusted Advisors understand financial planning isn't really about dollars and cents, bear and bull markets, stocks and bonds, tax breaks and inflation hedges. It's about the hopes, dreams, values, goals, and passions of their clients. It's about helping people make critical decisions, which bear consequences not only for their immediate family members, but also for their posterity. It's about helping people maximize their personal joy and societal contributions both during their lifetimes as well as long after they have passed.

Human life value is the most important concept a trusted advisor understands. The trusted advisor understands a client's economic value, or his long-term earnings potential, is only a small fraction of his true worth. Some advisors, using the human life value principle, believe they can accurately calculate the value of a person's worth. But trusted advisors understand the flaw in this thinking. I see my clients as multidimensional. For instance, one client may be a CEO, husband, father, friend, brother, role model, mentor, etc. Most advisors look at him as a "financial machine" only. It is impossible to replace the true value of a human life because it is so multidimensional. Therefore, a trusted advisor is very clear that human life value—in a comprehensive sense—is the most important asset of all.

The Trusted Advisor also understands that every single client is different, which means that each client needs different tools, products, strategies, and timelines to achieve their unique goals. In traditional planning, investment brokers sell their clients investments, life insurance salesmen sell life insurance, annuity salesmen sell annuities. Every salesman with a hammer believes their nail is the answer. But the Trusted Advisor is a full-services resource.

Just as a master mechanic understands every aspect of the engine, the Trusted Advisor understands the machinations of the entirety of financial planning. He asks the prospect a comprehensive set of questions to discover and diagnose what the client's specific objectives are. Then he designs a plan tailored to a client's individual needs. The Trusted Advisor usually has a network of financial specialists who he may consult if he is outside of his area of specific expertise.

Dan Sullivan, the creator of Strategic Coach, teaches

that "Questions are infinitely more valuable than answers." I believe this statement is profound, and I use the philosophy constantly with my clients. I believe my role is to help my clients discover the right answers for them rather than just telling them what they should do based on numbers or calculations. The right answers can only emerge when the right questions are asked. And the right answers, specific to each client, lead to the right recommendations.

There's a formula I follow with each client, as taught to me by my coach, Steve D'Annunzio, based on the acronym IDEA:

- **"I" is for Inviting.** Most advisors try to sell prospects on becoming their clients. They tell them everything they can do for the prospects with the hopes of convincing them to become their clients. But I believe this approach starts the relationship in the wrong way and helps advisors attract clients who they are not a good fit to work with, which causes both parties to ultimately lose. My philosophy is to invite prospects to explore what it means to be a client of mine so we can both determine if we are a good fit for each other.

- **"D" is for Diagnosis.** Clients are always drawn to the advisor who gives them the clearest diagnosis. (If you were sick, would you be attracted to a doctor who was unclear about your diagnosis or one who was clear about your diagnosis?) As a Trusted Advisor I must understand that while financial planning is a forensic experience for me, it is an emotional experience for the client. The questions I ask, along with the financial planning tools I use, help me come up with the right diagnosis.

- **"E" is for Education and Empowerment.** Once I have a clear diagnosis of my prospects' challenges and blind spots, then I need to educate them in a manner, which empowers them to make good decisions regarding how to solve these problems. The math- and science-based financial planning software I use help me do this with confidence, based on what actually happens in the real world, not hypothetical illustrations.

- **"A" is for Acceptance and Alignment.** In this final step prospective clients make a decision to align and accept recommendations. This is not about me imposing my ideas, values, and goals onto them, but rather co-creating the best future for them. This is not about me convincing or persuading them to take my recommended course of action, but rather about making their path so clear that they choose it.

Since I've mentioned financial software and planning tools I use to diagnose and recommend, let me say a word on that. So many advisors get totally enthralled with a financial planning system to the point where they believe the reason a client should do business with them is because of their "superior" financial planning system. But, while they can be profoundly useful, financial planning software and systems are not the end-all, be-all. I view them as simply "communication technology." No matter how powerful their mathematical calculations, they cannot calculate for the *context* of individual client's lives. Context makes all the difference between a successful financial plan and one that fails to produce the desired outcomes.

Again, for Trusted Advisors the focus is always on the client, not on the system or product. The systems are there to help clients deepen their understanding of key philosophies, which can help them lead better lives.

Using every tool and product available to me, my job is to protect my clients' goals, values, and dreams. Note that I didn't say my job is to protect their money. The money is simply a means to much bigger, more important ends. Money is worthless scraps of paper without the context of what people want it to do for them.

See, if my focus is on the money, then two things happen, which are all too common in traditional planning: 1) I go after the sale, rather than focusing on the mission, and 2) I take the standard planning approach of helping my clients accumulate money, helping them meet their objectives. If my ly help people accumulate, say, a a retirement account by age sixty-five, then it wouldn't matter what tool I used so long as I achieved that objective. It could be a 401(k), an IRA, stocks, bonds, or even CDs for that matter.

But what my clients want to do with their retirement funds makes a world of difference as to which products and strategies are appropriate. So my job is to figure out what my clients are trying to accomplish, and then use everything in my tool belt to help them accomplish their goals.

This reminds me of the young boy and his father who were shopping for a Mother's Day gift. The boy eagerly found toys and asked his father if they could buy them.

"No," came the reply, "we're shopping for a gift for Mommy today."

The boy quickly answered, "I think Mommy wants an action figure!"

Typical advisors are like that little boy—they think every client wants or needs whatever product they sell, or whichever one pays them the highest commission/fee. They're not focused on what their clients actually want, but rather on what benefits them.

One method I use in my quest to help clients get what they want is the CLUE method, developed by my friend, Kim Butler, a very gifted Trusted Advisor (www.partners4prosperity.com):

- **C = Control:** Start flowing money into an accoun

you control instead of away from yourself in accounts you don't control.

- **L = Liquidity:** Build wealth that can't be taken away from you because of market conditions (stocks, real estate, etc.).

- **U = Use:** Save money for later and purchase discretionary items now.

- **E = Equity:** Create an account where you benefit from leverage in a way that is better than paying cash, because losing cash is losing interest in an investment.

And as with all tools, methods, products, and strategies I use, the starting point of the CLUE method is the client's goals.

Life Insurance: Needs-Based Versus Human Life Value

Because Trusted Advisors understand that people, not money, are the real assets, they are proponents of permanent insurance based on the "human-life approach." This is in contrast with the "needs-based approach," which Investopedia defines as:

> A method of calculating how much life insurance is required by an individual/family to cover their needs (i.e. expenses). These include things like funeral expenses, legal fees, estate and gift taxes, business buyout costs, probate fees, medical deductibles,

emergency funds, mortgage expenses, rent, debt and loans, college, child care, private schooling, and maintenance costs. The needs approach contrasts the human-life approach.

The human-life approach is defined as:

> A method of calculating the amount of life insurance a family will need based on the financial loss the family would incur if the insured person were to pass away today. It is usually calculated by taking into account a number of factors including but not limited to the insured individual's age, gender, planned retirement age, occupation, annual wage, employment benefits, as well as the personal and financial information of the spouse and/or dependent children.

This is why, in many cases, I am adamantly opposed to term insurance, and the "buy term and invest the difference" (BTID) strategy. BTID proponents claim that term insurance premiums are cheaper than permanent policy premiums. This is true—but only for the early years. The cost of term insurance rises dramatically over time, versus permanent policy premiums, which remain the same over a person's lifetime. Term insurance rates get so high people are forced to drop them when they reach retirement age. In fact, when you analyze the costs of term insurance over a person's lifetime, you realize it's the most expensive life insurance.

Of course, to typical planners and pundits this isn't a problem, because the strategy is based on you dropping your coverage anyway as your assets build. The idea is that by retirement age you'll have enough assets to be "self-insured." Your kids are out of the house, you'll quit your job and your income will stop. So why would you possibly need life insurance?

And that is the difference: Trusted Advisors understand life insurance is to protect your human life value, not your income. Therefore, there is never a good reason to drop it. You *always* have human life value, whether or not you have job income. You have a family for whom you want to continue creating value long after you are gone. You have values you want to perpetuate. You have causes you want to support.

The Myth of "Self-Insurance"

The idea that you can be self-insured by accumulating a lot of money and other assets is an absolute joke. The purpose of insurance is to "indemnify" losses, which means 1) to compensate for damage or loss sustained, expense incurred, etc., and 2) to guard or secure against anticipated loss; give security against future damage or liability.

Suppose I have a million dollars in cash and my home, which is worth $500,000, burns down. Do I have enough money to rebuild my house? Yes. But what happens to my net worth by replacing the house with my cash? In that case I haven't insured or indemnified anything; my net worth has been slashed by more than half. True indemnification means that your net worth would remain the same even after catastrophic losses, because of insurance.

The purpose of life insurance is not just to replace your income but to replace your human life value to the greatest extent possible. Of course, money can't ever replace you, but it can go to the causes that you would support were you still alive. Les McGuire, an advisor who passed away in 2006, once wrote, "Producers are committed to creating maximum value in all situations, regardless of circumstance, and they manage their risk to near zero. Consumers think that risk means losing money; Producers know that risk refers to lost production, whether created in the past or yet to be created in the future. Producers reduce both risks to near zero." Life insurance is what helps you continue creating value and producing in the world even in the event of your death.

It's not about the money—it's about you and your human life value. You are the real asset, not your property or money. This is why Solomon Huebner wrote in his book, *The Economics of Life Insurance*, "Life insurance must not be regarded as an expense to be grudgingly borne. To the thoughtful policyholder, its creative aspects, by way of personal initiative and productiveness, much more than counterbalance the cost involved."

I sometimes hear people complain about insurance costs. But when you ask them how much insurance they would buy the day after a catastrophic event, the answer is obvious: "As much as I could get!" And with life insurance, you're betting on a certain event—you know you're going to die eventually. You know you have human life value. So why in the world would you ever want to drop your life insurance coverage?

As Garrett Gunderson, the author of *Killing Sacred Cows: Overcoming the Financial Myths that are Destroying Your Prosperity*, wrote:

> Contrary to what the traditional financial industry leads us to believe, insurance is not to protect property values. It is to protect human life value, which is the source and creator of all property value. Your home is worthless without people to value it. If your home burns down, it doesn't represent a loss of wood and brick. Countless people expended thought, time, labor, and energy to produce your home and if it burns down, all that human production is lost, or consumed. We can't get rid of the risk of fire, but we can indemnify, or mitigate, the risk of lost production through insurance.
>
> Producers don't insure houses and cars because the houses and cars have value; they insure their human life value as relates to their ability to produce value with material things.
>
> Realize that every material thing is nothing but a representation of human life value, and when material things are destroyed or consumed,

it represents a loss of human life value. Be a wise steward of both your material blessings and your human life value by carrying the maximum amount of insurance to protect against the risk of lost production.

Solomon Huebner knew what he was talking about. You are your most important asset—not your money. And it's my job as a Trusted Advisor to protect your human life value and help you achieve your specific objectives.

TRUSTED ADVISOR PRINCIPLE #5

THE TRUSTED ADVISOR IS A COACH, NOT A WAITER

> "Sometimes people don't want to hear the truth because they don't want their illusions destroyed."
> –FRIEDRICH NIETZSCHE

> "The key is not the will to win. Everybody has that. It is the will to prepare to win that is important."
> –COACH BOBBY KNIGHT

EARL WEAVER, former manager of the Baltimore Orioles, had a rule that no one could steal a base unless he gave the steal sign.

This ruling upset Reggie Jackson, who felt he knew the pitchers and catchers well enough to judge when he could steal. One day he decided to steal without a sign. He got a good jump off the pitcher and easily beat the throw to second base. As he shook the dirt from his uniform, he smiled with delight, feeling he had vindicated his judgment.

Weaver later took Jackson aside and explained why he hadn't given the steal sign. The next batter was Lee May, a major power hitter. Because first base was open, the opposing team intentionally walked May. The batter after May hadn't been strong against this pitcher, so Weaver had to send in a designated hitter. That left their team without the bench strength they might have needed later in the game.

Jackson had seen a stolen base as involving only the relationship between pitcher and catcher. Weaver was calling signals with the entire game in mind.

In my financial career I've had many experiences that can be compared to this story. For example, shortly after I got into the business in 1987 I started working with an executive of a Fortune 500 company. He was sixty-four years old and ready to retire.

At the time I was using traditional methods to determine if a person was ready for retirement. The executive and I agreed that if he were to earn 8 percent on his portfolio and if inflation were to average 3 percent annually, then he would be able to achieve his retirement objectives.

However, I told him I was concerned with the structure of his portfolio, which was 90 percent company stock. He responded he knew the company was in good shape and there was no need to diversify. I also told him I was concerned that he had no guaranteed retirement income and that he was going to be draining his current assets.

He didn't take my recommendations and he retired. Unfortunately, his company was not in as good of shape as he thought and the general markets were shaky as well. Shortly after he retired, his company stock dropped by over 40 percent, which meant his entire plan was doomed. But he still held out hope that things would turn around, so he didn't go back to work immediately. His stock never did recover, however, and he ended up having to go back to work at age seventy and had to work for ten more years.

I learned several things from this experience:

1. Guaranteed retirement income is vital, as is portfolio diversification.
2. It is impossible to accurately predict what rate of return a person will earn on their portfolio.
3. It is impossible to predict what inflation is going to be.
4. If a problem occurs, just waiting and hoping things will straighten themselves out is a critical mistake.
5. Most importantly, I learned I need to be a coach, not a waiter, to my clients.

Waiters simply take orders. Typical advisors are waiters. A prospect comes to see them and says she wants a certain amount of property and casualty insurance coverage. The advisor says "Okay" and gives her what she asks for.

In contrast, Trusted Advisors don't take orders; they make recommendations. Now, this may seem like it conflicts with what I've said in previous chapters about understanding what clients want to accomplish, rather than imposing my agenda on them. But understand there's a big difference between objectives and methods. I listen to clients and understand their objectives. It's my job to provide the tools and strategies to accomplish those objectives. They point where they want to go, I show them how to get there.

In the process, I have to be willing to tell my clients what they need to do even if they want to do something else. For example, if a client comes to me and says they want to retire on an income of $8,000 a month within twenty years and they want to use Variable Universal Life to accomplish that objective, I can't in good conscience sign them up with a VUL. That's what a waiter would do, but I'm a coach. I would tell the client that a VUL is far too risky and he couldn't depend on it to accomplish his objective. I would make recommendations on the products I trust to get him where he wants to go, and in his desired time frame.

Let me give you a few real examples from my career to make this more concrete for you. Several years ago, during the dotcom era, I had a client who was concerned his portfolio was not achieving the level of returns his friends were achieving. His portfolio was well diversified and had the proper asset allocation, but he was getting a bit jealous and greedy watching his friends make a lot of money in tech stocks. He wanted to follow suit and invest more of his money in technology stocks. In fact, he wanted to move 80 percent of his money into technology stocks. I told him I would not do this because I thought it could be potentially damaging to him. I told him that if he wanted to do this, he would need to move his money to another broker.

He eventually calmed down and took my advice. The dotcom bubble burst about four months later. Had I taken and fulfilled his order as a waiter, he would have lost over 50 percent of his portfolio. It would have put his children's education and his retirement in jeopardy.

Another client, an MD, wanted to invest a significant amount of money in a 529 plan to fund his children's education. This MD is one of the most brilliant men I know, and his wife is equally intelligent. I told him that while 529 plans have a few benefits (tax advantages), there were some risks he needed to be aware of. One of which is the money cannot be used for any other purpose than education. After carefully explaining his options, he decided to use another vehicle to fund his kid's education. It proved to be sound advice—both of his kids earned full scholarships to college and he didn't need to use the money he had set aside for them.

I also work with several professional athletes. They are always approached about investing in restaurants and other endeavors. My general counsel is to not invest in businesses you don't fully understand and can't be involved in. I have seen millions of dollars lost in these types of deals. So I generally tell my clients if they want to invest in these type things, they should find another advisor. I know I have saved my clients millions with this advice.

I provide similar advice to clients who bring me investments that seem too good to be true, which happens on a fairly regular basis (e.g. Executive Life Annuities, Stanford Financial CDs, 419 plans, charitable split-dollar plans, etc.). I've saved my clients millions as I've helped them avoid these schemes, which have all tanked.

I once worked with a young married couple with significant wealth whose attorney suggested that they buy second-to-die insurance inside an irrevocable life insurance trust. I explained to the clients the attorney was making a common recommendation but had not disclosed the risk to implementing his strategy.

Here are the problems I saw:

1. They were making an irrevocable decision at age thirty-five, which is generally way too early to make those kinds of decisions.
2. The strategy did not account for the risk of divorce.
3. It did not account for the risk of wealth erosion.
4. It did not account for the risk of one person dying early and the other dying many years later.

In this case, two of the four actually happened: 1) Their business virtually collapsed, which drastically reduced their wealth, and 2) They got divorced. Had they done what the attorney suggested, they would have wasted a bunch on money on something of little value. Instead, I coached them to buy individual policies. This built cash value, which helped them weather the tough time, and they were both able to leave the marriage with insurance in place.

Like Earl Weaver saw things that Reggie Jackson didn't see, I see things my clients don't see because of my nearly three decades in financial planning. I see the big picture. I understand the fine print. Using math and science, I can analyze how a strategy is designed to work in real life. I don't have to guess, conjecture, or hypothesize. I can help clients see and avoid financial cliffs in their lives. I can help them avoid pitfalls. But I can only do it when I act as a recommendation-making coach, not an order-taking waiter.

TRUSTED ADVISOR PRINCIPLE #6

THE TRUSTED ADVISOR IS A LIFELONG LEARNER

"The world is a university and everyone in it is a teacher. Make sure when you wake up in the morning you go to school."
—BISHOP T.D. JAKES

A young girl watched her mother prepare the ham for Easter dinner. The mother carefully cut each end off the ham before placing it in the pan.

"Mother," the child asked, "why do you always cut the ends off the ham?"

"Well, that's the way my mother always did it," her mother replied.

Her curiosity left unsatisfied, the child called her grandmother and asked, "Grandma, why do you always cut the ends off the ham?"

The grandmother replied, "Because that's the way my mother always did it."

Finally, the child called her great-grandmother and asked, "Great-Grandma, why did you always cut the ends off the ham?"

The great-grandmother replied, "Because the ham was way too big to fit in my small baking pan!"

That widely-told story is highly applicable to financial planning. Like any industry, financial planning is riddled with myths and false traditions, most of which arise from people not questioning common beliefs.

For example, why do most people think it's a great idea to save in 401(k)s? "Don't you know? Because my company matches my contributions, I get a 100 percent return—before my money ever goes into the market."

Yeah, I understand the match. I see you cutting off the ends of that ham with each contribution. But what the match-myth disguises is a very simple truth: *A return is not a return until it's realized.* Yes, a dollar-for-dollar company match does give you a 100 percent return on your money. At least it *would* were you to withdraw your money immediately after receiving the match. Unfortunately, you can't do that without being subject to penalties and taxes. So what would be your real return after that? Not even close to 100 percent.

And obviously, no one is doing that anyway. After receiving the match, of course, your 401(k) contributions are usually placed in market accounts, making them subject to market volatility. And if you don't withdraw the funds until retirement, then and only then can you calculate your return—after accounting for market fluctuations, fees, taxation, and inflation—which again is nowhere near 100 percent.

Trusted Advisors can help you see through the myths to make wiser financial decisions. But they can only help you do so if they've questioned traditional beliefs and exposed the myths themselves, which is the result of a dedication to lifelong learning.

Abraham Lincoln said, "If I had eight hours to chop down a tree, I'd spend seven sharpening my saw." Let's compare my role as an advisor to chopping down trees for my clients—in other words, helping them achieve their financial objectives. Using that analogy, the sharper I keep my saw, the faster and more effectively I can help my clients. Lifelong learning is how I continually sharpen my saw.

Like any Trusted Advisor, I have spent a lot of time learning my skill. Here is a short list of the things I have done to enhance my education.

- **Master of Science of Financial Services (MSFS):** This accredited, academic degree, requiring graduate courses, helps me analyze, plan, and implement integrated strategies in financial planning.
- **Certified Exit Planner (CExp):** I took a course that required 100+ hours of coursework to help my

business owner clients with complex exit strategy issues.

- **Certified in Trusts and Estates (CES):** Most of my clients have complex estate planning issues to deal with, and this designation helps me save my clients taxes, hassle, and heartache.

- **Certified Fund Specialist (CFS):** I secured this designation many years ago to increase my investment knowledge.

- **Senior Clients Training:** I have taken many courses to learn how to better work with senior clients.

I don't share my designations to brag, but rather to simply make the point that I understand I can never know it all and I can never learn enough. I attend educational workshops on a regular basis—and I spend a lot of money doing so. I'm an active member of the Association for Advanced Life Underwriting, which provides continuing education for members. Even though I've been working with IRAs for the past 27 years, I recently attended a two-day workshop on IRA planning to learn more about how to use IRAs for advanced applications. I spend a minimum of twenty days a year exploring new things to apply in my firm for our clients. A seminar about estate planning I recently attended totally changed the way I do estate planning—after doing estate planning for almost three decades.

I'm also dedicated to learning not just because there's so much to learn, but also because the rules are constantly changing in this business. For example, the Economic Growth and Tax Relief Reconciliation Act of 2001 took the first step in totally eliminating the death tax. It provided for a scheduled phase-out of rates and an increase in the unified credit, finally repealing the tax for calendar year 2010. Unfortunately, the provisions were set to sunset in 2011 and the estate tax would have reverted to the 1997 law with a top rate of 55 percent and a unified credit of $1,000,000. There was no estate tax in 2010. Congress then passed a two-year law, which brought the exemption up to $5 million per year. On Jan 1, 2013 these laws were made permanent. Essentially, from 2001 until 2013 there was no certainty as far as estate taxes were concerned.

In 1988 "modified endowments" were created in the Technical Corrections Act (H.R. 4333, S. 2238) in response to single-premium life (endowments) being used as tax shelters. The Act of 1988 established the Seven-Pay Test, which is a stipulated premium that would create a guaranteed paid-up policy within seven years from policy inception. If premiums paid to the contract go beyond (i.e. are higher than) the premium amount stipulated, then the contract has failed the Seven-Pay Test and is reclassified as a

Modified Endowment Contract. The following new tax rules apply to Modified Endowment Contracts:

- Distributions will switch from a First In First Out (FIFO) basis to a Last In First Out (LIFO) basis. This means that withdrawals will require the policy owner to withdraw taxable gain before withdrawing un-taxable basis.

- Policy loans will be realized as ordinary income to the policy owner and could be subject to income taxes in the year the loan is made.

- Distributions (either withdrawals or loans) that go beyond the policy basis will be subject to a 10 percent penalty tax for policy owners under the age of fifty-nine-and-a-half (this can be avoided by the use of a 72(v) distribution).

Once a contract has violated the Seven-Pay Test, the reclassification to a Modified Endowment Contract is irrevocable. Transferring funds from a Modified Endowment Contract to a new life insurance policy via the 1035 exchange privilege will render the newly-issued contract as Modified Endowment Contract as well.

Another legislative change now prohibits investor-owned life insurance (buying life insurance on a person you don't know for investment purposes). The current law is that insurable interest must be proven. Yet another example is dramatic changes that were made to split-dollar life insurance a few years ago, which caused a lot of issues for policyholders.

Many years ago I suffered a catastrophic knee injury. The doctor who performed my surgery was considered one of the best in the country and operated on many professional athletes. I used him because at the time he was widely-known as one of the best knee surgeons in the business. He used the most advanced techniques known at the time to repair my knee. I was in a cast for nine months. Today, surgeons are using completely different—and far superior—techniques, which make for much shorter recovery times. Were my doctor to use the same techniques today that he used on me years ago, he would lose his license.

It's funny this principle is so obvious in medicine, but not so obvious in financial planning. Most advisors get comfortable, and therefore stuck, with what they know, as long as it makes them money. I know many advisors who are doing the exact same things for clients today they were doing ten years ago—not because they are superior strategies, but because it's all they know. Many advisors never pursue professional designations. They do only what is required to keep their licenses.

It reminds me of high jumping. Before 1968, all high jumpers used very rudimentary techniques to clear the bar, most commonly the "straddle technique" or the Western Roll. But in 1965, Dick Fosbury began experimenting and developed what is now known as the "Fosbury Flop," which consists of flying backwards over the bar and landing on one's back on the mat. At first, Fosbury was ridiculed, his technique was ignored. But that all changed when he won the gold medal for high jump in the 1968 Olympics. Now, the Fosbury Flop is the exclusive technique used by high jumpers worldwide. It's considered the obvious and only way to do it. But that wasn't the case before one man chose to question tradition and experiment with different techniques.

Like Dick Fosbury, Trusted Advisors have an insatiable hunger to learn how to be better at their craft. They have a willingness to challenge what they do and how they do it. They're constantly asking themselves, "Is this the best way to do this?" They're never content with the status quo. They're always innovating and experimenting.

Of course, no client wants an advisor to experiment with his or her money. That's why Trusted Advisors experiment the same way scientists do—in the lab. Using the right software, it's actually quite easy to map out scenarios and play out "what ifs" without ever using actual money. We seek to know whether or not a product or strategy can work in the real world by applying rigorous tests in the lab.

Beware the Know-It-Alls

As counterintuitive as it sounds, one of the most comforting things you can ever hear a financial planner say is, "I don't know."

There's no way any advisor could possibly know everything there is to know about this business. It's far too complex. There are way too many products, strategies, and rules to learn. If an advisor appears to be a know-it-all, it should be a huge red flag to you; most likely, he is bluffing his way through things he doesn't really know or understand.

The Trusted Advisor isn't blinded by hubris. Neither does he fly solo. I have a network of other advisors who have expertise in areas in which I am not as comfortable. For example, I am not a pension expert or skilled at group health insurance so I have resources in both of those arenas.

There are four realms of knowledge:

1. The things you know that you know.
2. The things you think you know.
3. The things that you know that you don't know.
4. The things that you don't know that you don't know.

It's that fourth realm which gets both investors and advisors into trouble. The Trusted Advisor gives great recommendation when she operates from the first realm, and she's constantly trying to expand that realm through lifelong learning. She is also humble enough to admit when she's entered into the second and third realms. Typical advisors stumble into holes and expose you to pitfalls by trying to be know-it-alls from that fourth realm.

Three Traditional Investment Myths Exposed

Much of the next chapter is going to be my attempt to shed light on proper investing instead of what I see most people doing, which I refer to as speculating and gambling. Before I go further I would like to give credit to Mark Matson, a financial advisor and founder of Matson Money (www.matsonmoney), for his coaching. The information below, which comes from his research, is shared with his permission.

One of the first things Mark taught me was what he refers to as the three investment myths and I now want to share them with you as they are instrumental in you becoming a good investor. The Three Myths are:

1. Myth #1: Stock Selection
2. Myth #2: Track-Record Investing
3. Myth #3: Market Timing

Myth #1: Stock Selection

THE MYTH: Investment professionals can consistently and predictably add value by exercising "superior skill" in individual stock selection.

Most people don't realize that many mutual funds are closed or get merged with other funds. When that happens, the returns data for those funds disappear. Data from the Center for Research in Securities Prices at the University of Chicago, which shows all "live" and "dead" funds, reveals some very interesting things.

Year	Number of Funds	Number of New Funds	Number of Dead Funds	Year	Number of Funds	Number of New Funds	Number of Dead Funds
1923	1	1	0	1970	603	71	23
1924	4	3	0	1971	619	48	32
1925	5	1	0	1972	616	32	35
1926	6	1	0	1973	609	29	36
1927	6	1	0	1974	596	34	47
1928	10	4	0	1975	590	25	31
1929	16	6	0	1976	613	48	25
1930	17	1	0	1977	639	53	27
1931	21	4	0	1978	652	39	26
1932	37	16	0	1979	678	51	25
1933	46	9	0	1980	732	74	20
1934	48	2	0	1981	862	146	16
1935	57	9	0	1982	1043	205	24
1936	59	2	0	1983	1231	213	25
1937	62	3	0	1984	1471	259	19
1938	71	9	0	1985	1816	362	17
1939	78	7	0	1986	2266	474	24
1940	86	8	0	1987	2779	548	35
1941	87	1	0	1988	3165	466	80
1942	87	0	0	1989	3377	330	118
1943	87	0	0	1990	3682	491	186
1944	93	6	0	1991	4177	610	115
1945	98	5	0	1992	5061	1056	172
1946	103	5	0	1993	6756	1855	160
1947	113	10	0	1994	8739	2216	233
1948	117	4	0	1995	9890	1643	492
1949	130	13	0	1996	11205	1822	507
1950	137	7	0	1997	12903	2231	533
1951	142	5	0	1998	14398	2165	670
1952	152	10	0	1999	16069	2187	516
1953	163	11	0	2000	17993	2863	939
1954	183	20	0	2001	19448	2483	1028
1955	186	3	0	2002	20603	2427	1272
1956	205	19	0	2003	21264	1877	1216
1957	222	17	0	2004	22264	1981	981
1958	241	19	0	2005	23525	2397	1136
1959	267	26	0	2006	25234	2786	1077
1960	281	14	0	2007	26353	2720	1601
1961	273	25	33	2008	27562	2787	1578
1962	285	12	0	2009	26721	1767	2608
1963	296	11	0	2010	27537	2380	1564
1964	312	16	0	2011	28319	2453	1671

Year	Number of Funds	Number of New Funds	Number of Dead Funds	Year	Number of Funds	Number of New Funds	Number of Dead Funds
1965	331	19	0	2012	29152	2339	1506
1966	360	29	0	Not defined	29370	265	47
1967	390	30	0				
1968	463	74	0	Total	29370	51905	22535
1969	555	100	8				

For illustrative purposes only. Mutual fund data provided by CRSP Survivor Bias Free Mutual Fund Database. CRSP data provided by the Center for Research in Security Prices, University of Chicago. 12/31/2012

In 2012 there were 29,152 open mutual funds, which is over three times as many funds as there are publicly-traded stocks in the U.S. market. Between 1923 and 2012, a total of 51,905 mutual funds were opened. If there are currently only about 29,000 funds open, how many of the nearly 52,000 funds were closed? *A staggering 22,535.*

Why do you suppose the funds disappeared? And what happened to the return statistics for those killed funds?

The average return for the 200 worst-performing mutual funds in history is negative 79.3 percent. Are you starting to figure out why the mutual fund industry would want to kill these funds, and then hide their data? Significantly underperforming funds are quietly closed and merged into more successful funds. This allows the mutual fund companies to post better returns, essentially sweeping bad performers under the rug. You have to ask yourself, if fund managers are so great at picking stocks, why are so many funds being closed due to atrocious performance? It's like your son bringing home his report card and reporting that he got straight A's, while failing to mention that he actually failed three classes, but those grades had been removed from his report card.

So let's look at the long-term impact of active stock management. Consider the chart below. The —-- line shows the return of a $100,000 investment in the average of the U.S. equity mutual funds since 1972. Keep in mind that stocks within these mutual funds are actively traded by the smartest fund managers. The ····· line shows a completely passive approach to investing, putting $100,000 in the S&P 500 Index in 1972.

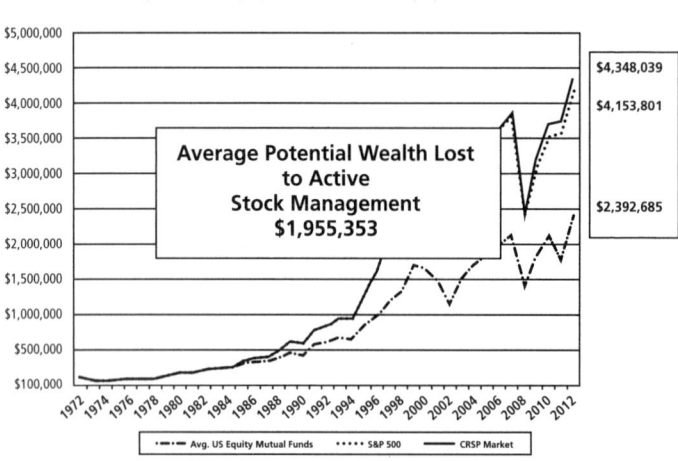

Data representing the average of all US equity mutual funds, the S&P 500 Index and the CRSP Market Index were extracted from returns software provided by Dimensional Fund Advisors (DFA). The referenced indices are discussed in more detail in the endnotes. Average fund performance results and comparative indices assume reinvestment of dividends and income. Average fund data also includes fund expense ratios associated with active management, but does not include sales commissions; however, the indices are unmanaged, cannot be invested in directly and their returns do not reflect any management fees, transaction costs or expenses. This graph does not reflect actual investor results and no representation is made that your portfolio would experience similar results. Past performance is no guarantee of future success.

The difference between the actively-traded approach versus the passive index approach is a staggering $1,955,353. This isn't speculation or projections. This is math and science proving that actively picking stocks does not work. To put it bluntly, anyone who thinks they can increase their returns from picking stocks and predicting the market is blind, foolhardy, and frankly arrogant.

Myth #2: Track-Record Investing

THE MYTH: Finding funds that did well in the past is a reliable method of indicating which funds will do well in the future.

Let's consider the top thirty mutual funds during the ten-year period from 1993 to 2002. Compared to all funds, the S&P and the U.S. market as a whole, these thirty funds delivered significantly higher returns.

	1993-2002
Top 30 US Equity Funds Average Annual Return	25.64%
All US Equity Funds Average Annual Return	16.00%
S&P 500 Average Annual Return	11.18%
CRSP 1-10 Average Annual Return	10.64%
Total # of US Equity Funds Survivinig 1993-2002	725
Total # of US Equity Funds Surviving 203-212	

Which funds do you think most financial advisors were recommending in January 2003? Yep, you guessed it—it looked like a list of these funds.

Here's a little known fact that mutual fund companies probably don't want you to know about that ten-year period. Out of the entire universe of 1,817 U.S. equity mutual funds that were open January 1, 1993, only 725 had a ten-year track record at END of the ten-year period.

Now let's see how these top thirty funds did in the following ten-year period:

	1993-2002	2003-2012
Top 30 US Equity Funds Average Annual Return	25.64%	0.18%
All US Equity Funds Average Annual Return	16.00%	2.83%
S&P 500 Average Annual Return	11.18%	8.84%
CRSP 1-10 Average Annual Return	10.64%	9.78%
Total # of US Equity Funds Survivinig 1993-2002	725	
Total # of US Equity Funds Surviving 203-212		3738

For illustrative purposes only. Mutual funds data provided by CRSP Survivor-Bias Free Mutual Fund Database, includes funds that are U.S. Equity mutual funds. The S&P data are provided by Standard & Poor's Index Services Group. CRSP data provided by the Center for Research in Security Prices, University of Chicago. Indices are not available for direct investment, therefore their performance does not reflect the expenses associated with the management of an actual portfolio.

Did they repeat the performance? Nope—they actually underperformed both the Average Fund, the S&P Index, and the market as a whole. What's worse, once you realized they weren't doing as well as you had expected them to do, there were even more funds out there to choose from in your search for an alternative.

And, here again, we see the same curious phenomenon in the survivorship of mutual funds. Only 3,738 funds with ten years of history managed to stay open from the beginning of 2003 through the end of 2012. As we saw on a previous slide, even after "killing off" some 22,000 funds, there were still over 29,000 funds in existence in 2012. And how many do you suppose will still be alive ten years from now? And how in the world would we be able to identify the best ones *in advance*? Keep in mind what happens to the returns statistics for the funds that "die."

The point is this: A fund manager's ability to pick stocks in the past has zero correlation with his or her ability to do so in the future.

Think of it this way: Imagine you put 100 people in a room, and you have them all flip quarters. You have everyone who gets tails sit down. After several rounds of this, eventually you'll end up with just a couple of people still standing. Now, were you to have everyone stand up and go through the exercise again, would you bet on those same people winning again? Would you bet your entire future on that outcome? Obviously not.

But that's exactly what happens with track-record investing—it's nothing more than a coin toss. Fund managers and/or individual investors are trying to predict future returns based on past results. It's ludicrous.

Myth #3 Market Timing

THE MYTH: Money managers are able to utilize market timing to effectively predict up and down markets.

How easy do you think it is to get in and out of the market at the right time?

Well, let's look at a study done by DALBAR, an independent research firm that does massive studies on investor behavior—the real results that investors get. After concluding a twenty-year study of tens of thousands of brokerage accounts for investors who have over $100,000 invested, here's what they found:

Category	1993-2012 Annualized Return
S&P 500 Index	8.21%
Dalbar Average Investor – Equity Fund	4.25%
CPI (representing Inflation)	2.43%

DALBAR, Inc., Quantitative Analysis of Investor Behavior, 2013

During the time period, the S&P 500 Index returned 8.21 percent, while the average investor only received a 4.25 percent return. But when you add inflation to the mix, the investors only realized a 1.82 percent return.

The point is that market timing is risky and it simply doesn't work. Missing the market's top-performing days can prove costly. This chart shows how a $10,000 investment would have been affected by missing the market's top-performing days over the twenty-year period from July 1, 1993 to June 30, 2013:

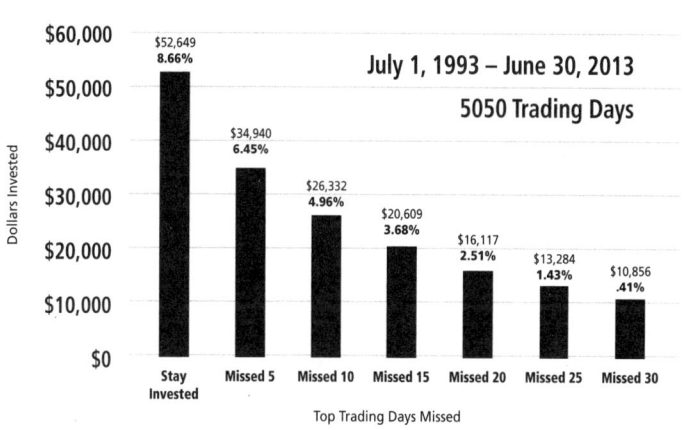

Growth of a $10,000 Investment

Source: ChartSource®, McGraw-Hill Financial Communications. For the period from July 1, 1993 – June 30, 2013. Based on total returns of Standard & Poor's Composite Index of 500 Stocks, an unmanaged index that in generally considered representative of the U.S. stock market. It is not possible to invest directly in an index. Past performance is not a guarantee of future results. Copyright © 2011, McGraw-Hill Financial Communications. All rights reserved. Not responsible for any errors or omissions. Based on initial investment of $10,000.

> "The evidence on investment managers' success with market timing is impressive - and overwhelmingly negative." –Charles D. Ellis, Investment Policy, 1993

For example, an individual who remained invested for the entire time period would have accumulated $44,087 over the period, while an investor who missed just the ten top-performing days during that period would have accumulated only $22,050—nearly half as much! There are 5,040 trading days. If you only miss ten of the best ones, you get less than what you would have traditionally earned in a simple T-Bill.

Clearly, traditional investment strategies of stock selection, track record investing, and market timing have all been proven empirically to not be effective investing methods. They aren't predictable, they aren't repeatable, and they're forms of speculation.

These are just three myths of many to make the point that many investors and advisors think they know what they're doing when they try to pick stocks and time the market, among other strategies. But as Mark Twain said, "It ain't what you don't know that gets you into trouble. It's what you know for sure that just ain't so."

The Trusted Advisor doesn't blindly follow the herd. He doesn't accept trite sayings, no matter how often they're repeated or how many people say them. He's constantly learning to see the reality behind myths.

The 10,000 Hour Rule

In his fascinating book, *Outliers*, journalist and thought leader Malcolm Gladwell analyzes the lives of extremely successful people to identify the factors that contribute to world-class success in any field or endeavor. His most widely-published conclusion is that it takes about 10,000 hours of practice to achieve mastery in a field.

His hypothesis is supported by many studies. For example, in the early 1990s, a team of psychologists in Berlin, Germany studied the practice habits of violin students in childhood, adolescence, and adulthood. All of the subjects were asked, "Over the course of your entire career, ever since you first picked up the violin, how many hours have you practiced?" All of the violinists had begun playing at roughly five years of age with similar practice times. However, at age eight, practice times began to diverge. By age twenty, the elite performers averaged more than 10,000 hours of practice each, while the less able performers had only 4,000 hours of practice. The elite had more than double the practice hours of the less capable performers.

Gladwell explains that reaching the 10,000-hour rule is simply a matter of practicing a specific task that can be accomplished with twenty hours of work a week for ten years.

I believe this rule holds true for financial planning. Ideally, the Trusted Advisor has crossed the 10,000-hour barrier two or three times. But understand, this may not necessarily translate into years spent in the business. I've known advisors who have been in the business for thirty years, and I had more appointments with clients and prospects within three years than they have had throughout their career. What matters is hours spent truly working with clients, finding and implementing solutions to specific problems, learning new strategies and skills.

Of course, it presents a bit of a chicken-and-egg conundrum: How does an advisor get his 10,000 hours without meeting with clients? And how does he get clients before getting his hours in and becoming world-class? As with any technical profession, mentorship is critical. The two people who brought me into this business were both Certified Financial Planners, and they both played critical roles in my early training. One of them reviewed every financial plan I developed and made recommendations on how to improve each plan. The other was more involved with classroom training but her role was vital in helping me learn the fundamentals of the business. Their expertise was working with middle-income families.

After working with them a few years, I started to realize I was getting a lot of clients in the affluent marketplace. I did joint work with other producers in this market. While doing this, I also secured an estate planning designation. In this case, I actually brought the experienced estate planners to work with my clients while I watched and learned. After doing this quite a few times, I knew I was ready to begin to do it on my own.

The typical advisor has five to ten meetings per week. I was able to run fifteen to eighteen per week. I have found the best way to learn is to be face-to-face with clients. The key is when you don't know something to be honest and say, "That's not my area of expertise and I will bring someone in who specializes in this area." For example, when I had a client who wanted to implement a 401(k) in his business, I had no expertise in the field so I brought in a 401(k) specialist to learn from.

You can certainly work with a younger advisor, just as long as he or she works closely with an experienced Trusted Advisor and is humble and honest enough to admit when he or she needs help. You should never be concerned when an advisor admits he or she need help—in fact, that should increase your confidence in him or her. Because ultimately, humility is a sign of a hunger to learn, and that's one of the most important characteristics a Trusted Advisor can have.

CONCLUSION

HOW TO FIND A TRUSTED ADVISOR

> "The quality of any advice anybody has to offer has to be judged against the quality of life they actually lead."
> –DOUGLAS ADAMS

THE STORY IS TOLD of a young man who went to work for a rancher. The first day of work the rancher asked the man, "Can you sleep when the wind blows?" The young man was confused and didn't know what the rancher meant.

That night a severe storm woke up the young man and he jumped frantically out of bed, afraid that the cows would be lost in the storm. He ran outside, only to find that the cows were safe and warm inside the secure barn. The rancher had taken care of them before retiring for the night. As he went back inside, the man saw the rancher sleeping soundly, and he then knew the meaning of the question the rancher had asked.

When it comes to your money, are you like that young

man, or like the old rancher? Can you sleep when the wind blows? You can when you have a Trusted Advisor in your corner, helping you to avoid threats, fulfill obligations, and exploit opportunities.

By now you should already have a very clear idea of what to look for in an advisor. But to make the task simpler, here's a list of questions that can be used to interview prospective advisors and to help you identify what to look for:

- **How long have you been in the business?**

Ideally, the answer you're looking for here is at least ten years. If they have less than ten years of experience, then ask them whether or not they work closely with a more experienced advisor. Then, use the questionnaire to interview the experienced advisor to identify whether or not he or she is a Trusted Advisor.

- **Do you have any professional designations? If so, which ones, and will you explain what they mean?**

If she has none, that's a clear sign you shouldn't work with her.

- **What licenses do you hold?**

He should be able to list at least a couple. If he isn't investment licensed, he still may be appropriate to work with for your insurance needs.

- **Are you a member of any professional associations? If so, which ones and why?**

A Trusted Advisor should be able to list several.

- **Other than what is required to keep your licenses, what do you do to keep current in your industry?**

Someone who only does the minimum required continuing education is not a Trusted Advisor. A Trusted Advisor will be able to list a number of educational seminars and events she attends. Ask her to tell you about the last meeting she attended.

- **Are you in a study group of your peers?**

Most Trusted Advisors will answer "yes" to this question. If you get that answer, ask him to tell you about the group and look for accomplishments and credentials from the members.

- **Are you able to show me, using math and science, whether or not your recommendations will work in the real world, or will you just be presenting hypothetical illustrations that are not based on actual market performance?**

The best answer here would be that the advisor uses a number of different software programs that help him base his recommendations on math and science. If he answers that his recommendations are based on math and science versus hypothetical projections, ask him to show you an example.

- **Are your illustrations based on projections of future market performance? If so, what rate of return do you use in your illustrations?**

If she answers "yes" to this question, that alone tells you she's not a Trusted Advisor. And you especially know she's not if the answer to the follow-up question is anything higher than a 5 percent consistent projected annual return.

- **What is my greatest asset?**

The answer you're looking for here is, "You are." Remember: You're looking for an advisor who protects your Human Life Value first and foremost, your material assets second.

- **Do you use the same products and strategies you recommend to clients?**

In addition to learning whether or not he takes his own recommendations, you also want to get a feel for his personal financial situation. Remember: A desperate advisor can never be objective about your situation and will usually just go after the highest commission, versus what is in your best interest.

- **Do you recommend the same products and strategies to every client, or do you provide customized recommendations for each client?**

Very few advisors are going to admit that they give the same things to every client. So if she answers that she provides customized recommendations, ask her to give you very specific examples.

- **Do you have favorite companies you write business with?**

"Yes" is an acceptable answer. In that case, get the list and check their financial ratings. If they are not highly rated, the advisor may be writing business with the carrier for higher commissions.

- **Can you show me an example of a financial plan you put together for a client?**

"Yes" is obviously the right answer here. Any financial advisor should be able to provide this. When he presents the plan and shares the rationale behind his recommendations, listen to his explanations to identify the elements we've discussed in this book. For example, were his recommendations based on math and science, or hypothetical illustrations?

- **Do you believe that 401(k)s provide tax savings?**

If he answers "yes," you know with certainty that he doesn't know what he's talking about. The accurate answer is, "It depends."

- **Is there any fine print in any of the products you recommend that I should be aware of?**

Every financial product has fine print you should be aware of.

- **Have you ever answered "I don't know" to any question asked by a prospect or client?**

Ideal answer? "Yes, all the time." Ask her to provide specific examples, and what she does when she doesn't know the answer to something.

- **Have you ever fired a client? If so, why?**

This question is designed to help you ascertain whether the advisor acts as a coach or as a waiter. Waiters would never dream of firing clients—they simply do what the clients tell them to do without question. Coaches, on the other hand, will respectfully but firmly invite clients to work with another advisor if they insist on doing things that will be harmful to them.

- **If I told you exactly what financial product I wanted, would you sell it to me?**

The answer you're looking for here is, "I would never sell anything to any client without first understanding their situation in detail."

AFTERWORD

LESSONS ON SUCCEEDING FINANCIALLY FROM MY SUMMIT OF MT. KILIMANJARO

> "When it is obvious that the goals cannot be reached, don't adjust the goals, adjust the action steps."
> —CONFUCIUS

WHEN I WAS TWENTY-FOUR YEARS OLD, I heard Lou Holtz speak, and it had a huge impact on my life. During his speech he recommended that we write down 100 things we want to accomplish in our life. As you know, years later a movie was made titled *The Bucket List*, but I first heard the idea from Coach Holtz.

In 1979, a study, which analyzed MBA students, proved the wisdom of Holtz's advice. The study asked participants one simple question: "Have you set clear, written goals for your future and made plans to accomplish them?" The research discovered that:

- 3 percent of the class had written goals and plans
- 13 percent had unwritten goals
- 84 percent had no goals at all

Ten years later, the group of 3 percent with written goals had a higher net worth than the other 97 percent combined! Even more incredible, the 3 percent with written goals and plans earned ten times as much as all the others put together. The 13 percent with unwritten goals earned twice as much as the 84 percent with no goals. It's a fact: People who have clear and compelling goals—especially written ones—are far more likely to succeed than those who don't.

Well, when I heard Coach Holtz speak I didn't know the research data. But I thought it sounded like a good idea, so I started my list. The process I've gone through teaches a lot of valuable lessons for anyone wanting to succeed financially.

It took a few days to complete but I finally got to 100. I had no clue how much impact this exercise would later have on my life. (By the way, climbing Mount Kilimanjaro was number fifty-seven on my list.)

By the time I reached age fifty-five, I realized that I had accomplished almost everything on my original list of 100. (The list has continued to grow substantially over the years.) But on my fifty-fifth birthday, I reviewed my bucket list. Climbing Mount Kilimanjaro, which I hadn't given much thought to for more than thirty years, stuck out like a sore thumb. It spoke to me.

I wouldn't take much action on that goal, however, until a few weeks later when I met with a group of friends for dinner and one of them started telling me about his recently-completed summit of Mt. Kilimanjaro. I peppered him with questions about his adventure. That night I decided to get serious about my goal.

I have a very defined process for accomplishing goals, and I used that process for this trek. **The first step in my process is to write the goal down.** In this case, I wrote this statement: "I will summit Mount Kilimanjaro in the spring of 2014." That was in May of 2013.

The second step in my process is to write down all of the potential obstacles that may prevent me from accomplishing the goal. In the case of this trek, my list was long:

- Was my general health good enough to complete the trek? I had just turned 55 years old and hadn't had a physical in years.

- Could I overcome some serious orthopedic issues? I had a catastrophic knee injury while in college and have had multiple knee surgeries since the original surgery. I have acute osteoarthritis in my right knee.

- Could I overcome my lack of hiking experience? At the time I planned the trip, I had never been on a hike or camped.
- I live at sea level and the summit of Kilimanjaro is at 19,341 feet. The number one reason for failure to summit is altitude sickness.
- Was my physical fitness good enough to do the hike? I worked out with weights regularly, but my cardio is very limited because of my knee issue.
- I had no clue what the total cost of the trip would be, so I obviously needed to see if this is something I wanted to afford.
- I didn't know which trekking company to hire.
- I had no hiking or camping gear.
- Kilimanjaro is in a developing country, so infectious diseases are present.

The third step in my process is to develop an action plan to deal with each of the potential obstacles. Here are the steps I took to deal with the aforementioned obstacles:

- I met with my MD, Liza Leal. She performed a general physical and said I was in excellent condition. She referred me to a cardiologist, Dr. Kota Reddy. He ran a complete battery of tests and told me my heart was in great shape. She referred me to an MD, Dr. Edward Rensimer, who specializes in Travel Medicine. He made several recommendations that included vaccinations and one medication, Diamox, to deal with the potential of altitude sickness.

- I met with my orthopedist, Dr. Vishal Shah. He recommended I get Synvisc injections in both of my knees to act as artificial cartilage, which I did.

- I hired a guide to take me on a five-hour hike while I was attending a meeting in Phoenix several months before the trip. I learned the basics of hiking on this hike. (I wish I had had the opportunity to do more hiking, as it would have made my experience more enjoyable.)

- I researched altitude sickness and altitude training. As a result of this research, I purchased a machine which helps train you for dealing with altitude. I used the machine for thirty days before the trek as per the instructions.

- I hired a company, Fit for Trips, to design a fitness plan for me.

- I did a lot of research to find the trekking company. I decided on Thomson Safaris as they appeared to be a first-class operation and they answered all of my questions and made gave me detailed recommendations.

The fourth step in my process is to adapt to

unknown obstacles as they present themselves. I have never accomplished a goal without having to adapt the plan along the way. In the case of this trip, I had to adapt a lot.

- I started doing the workouts recommended by Fit for Trips, but was unable to do some of the exercises because of my knee. I called Fit for Trips and they made suggestions to deal with my knee issue.

- Six months before the trip, I developed a severe case of Plantar Fasciitis in my right foot. This is an extremely painful condition that makes training almost impossible. I saw a podiatrist who helped me deal with the condition using orthotics, injections, and physical therapy.

- I also sought the help of a chiropractor who specializes in treating issues like Plantar Fasciitis.

- I adapted my training to put less pressure on my foot. I rode the stationary bike until I couldn't stand it anymore.

- My biggest obstacle happened the Sunday prior to my trip starting on the next Thursday. On Saturday night I did my altitude-training machine for about an hour and then my wife and I went out for a nice dinner. Before going to dinner, I took an energy supplement, as I was very tired. At dinner, we shared a bottle of wine. The next morning my resting heart rate was 144 instead of my normal 56 to 60 beats per minute. When this did not subside, I had my wife take me to an emergency hospital. The diagnosis was atrial fibrillation. The attending MD explained the condition and told me they were going to have to shock my heart to get it back in normal rhythm. He also said I could forget about my trek. I told the MD I was not comfortable having the procedure performed without talking to my cardiologist. He agreed and I immediately starting trying to get in touch with Dr. Reddy. Within twenty minutes, he called me back. I explained what I believed caused the problem (alcohol, energy drink, and altitude machine). His confident response was, "Let them do the procedure and be in my office on Monday morning. I know what caused the problem and I know how to prevent it and by the way you are going to climb Kilimanjaro." I must tell you, having my heart shocked was the scariest thing I have ever done, as the medical team was standing ready to start chest compressions and to ventilate if my heart were to have stopped. Fortunately, my heart started and was fine after the most violent thing I have ever felt. I went to see Dr. Reddy the next day and he performed several tests. We agreed on what I needed to do to go on the trek, and I left his office feeling very happy and surprisingly confident.

The fifth step in my process is to enjoy the journey and pay attention as things change. Following are some of the things I took away from the mountain, which I believe will help you on your journey to financial success.

During our initial trek briefing, our lead guide, Andrew, told us to forget about climbing Kilimanjaro. He said, "If you look at the mountain and its enormity, you will become discouraged. I want you to concentrate on two things: First, 'poli poli,' which means 'slowly, slowly,' in Swahili, and second, concentrate on your next step only." He said by doing this we would have the energy to climb the mountain safely and the emotional strength to endure its rigors. Andrew also told us we would get discouraged along the way and we should just keep confident and take the next step. (I think Andrew would be an excellent retirement planner as his advice is particularly adaptable to planning for the enormity of planning for retirement.)

The average daily hiking time on our trek was seven to nine hours a day. I experienced moments of doubt along the way. When I doubted myself, I just focused on taking the next step. I would also take a moment to enjoy the beauty of the mountain. There is nothing like waking up at 15,000 feet to a warm cup of coffee and the view of the clouds below you.

My final lesson, learned on the day of our summit attempt, is a valuable lesson for everyone. The hike the day of the summit starts at about 6 a.m., and it is a grueling hike. There were several times during the day when I doubted my ability to summit. But I kept hearing Andrew's words: "Next step. Poli poli. Next step." At about 4 p.m., I reached the summit. It was one of the greatest feelings in the world. I was elated and moved to tears.

Little did I know the mountain had one final lesson it wanted to give me. As I started down the mountain, I began to realize how unstable the ground was and how hard it was on my knees. Every step was painful, and, after the first hour, made in darkness. After two hours of absolute misery and with very little energy left in my tank (I didn't eat enough), I saw the flickering lights of camp. I told myself, "You got this. Only thirty more minutes." Two hours later we were still hiking and I began to lose it physically and emotionally.

It took every bit of my strength to take the next step. There were times when I was in tears. I finally arrived in camp fifteen hours after my summit journey began. When I woke up the next morning, I reflected on what went wrong on the way down. I concluded that I had ungrounded expectations, and then became discouraged when they were not met. I could have grounded my expectations if I had asked one question of my Trusted Advisor when I saw camp: "How far is camp?"

I hope you won't think I'm self-indulgent to share that story with you. My point in sharing it is that this experience is much like your experience with building long-term wealth. Here are a few lessons I hope you take from this story:

- If you don't have written financial goals, I urge you to create some and write them down. After all, if you don't know where you want to go, how can you expect a Trusted Advisor to get you there?

- Once you have written goals, then take them through the process. Identify your potential obstacles. Create plans for dealing with those obstacles. Adapt to unknown obstacles as they present themselves.

- Don't forget to enjoy the journey along the way. Don't scrimp and save so much that your accumulation period is miserable. Remember that it's not money that you want—it's the experiences that money can buy.

- Finally, and most importantly, make sure you have a Trusted Advisor who can help you put one foot in front of the other, coach you through the entire journey, and help you reach your destination.

MY INVITATION TO YOU

Thanks for taking the time to read my book. I am honored that you would invest your valuable time to read it, and I hope you found it useful.

As I mentioned earlier, the first step in my work with prospective clients is to invite them to explore what it means to be a client of mine so we can both determine if we are a good fit for each other. This meeting is strictly an exploratory meeting to help me determine if I can make a difference in your life. I tell all of my prospective clients to leave their checkbooks at home as no recommendations will be made.

I invite you to schedule an appointment with me. The easiest way to do so is to call or email me directly at (832) 600-1531 or rickray@wealthdesigngroup.net.

APPENDIX

Belief Statements for Wealth Design Group, LLC

PURPOSE – We exist to educate and empower people with customized wealth plans that provide them with enduring confidence and financial success.

MISSION – We invite caring individuals, families, and business owners to meet us and learn about our unique wealth-building philosophy and process.

1. We believe our purpose in business is to improve the welfare of humanity, one family at a time.
2. We believe people are the primary asset, so our primary focus is serving all stakeholders we affect: clients, employees, employers, and everyone in our community.
3. We believe only by putting our clients' needs and wants first can we sustain ongoing company growth and profitability.
4. We believe the reason for our innovation and creativity is to enhance the complete value of human life.
5. We believe any financial planning conversation must initially focus on protecting the financial value of each human life.
6. We believe we have a duty to identify and help

resolve unseen money issues, which can cause a multitude of family conflicts.

7. *We believe there are thousands of caring people needing our services, and it is our job to reach out and offer to serve them in a timely and proactive manner.*
8. *We believe by utilizing a principled approach to wealth management and planning we can co-design enduring financial legacies with our clients.*
9. *We celebrate the accomplishment of individuals while recognizing the power of our team.*
10. *We believe in ongoing education to improve continually and master our craft.*
11. *We believe we are engaged in a noble profession of success through service. We always seek to enroll and support new people who are ready to learn, work, and grow.*

ACKNOWLEDGMENTS

My heartfelt thanks goes to the following individuals, without whom I would never be successful and this book would have never been produced:

My parents, Mary Margaret Ray and MD Ray, for your unconditional love and unwavering confidence in me. You taught me the value of hard work, dedication, and pursuing my dreams passionately.

My wife, Tara, for your love and for allowing me to pursue my dreams. You have been my partner in life and in business for more than two decades and I could not have achieved what I have without you.

My children, Jordan and Micayla, for allowing me to love and guide you. Jordan, you have taught me more than you will ever know. Micayla, your enthusiasm for life is infectious and makes me smile.

My friend and mentor, Steve D'Annunzio, for encouraging me to write this book. The lessons you have taught me have helped me become a better man, both personally and professionally.

Gail Winfree, for bringing me into this wonderful industry many years ago. Most of my friends and family thought I was crazy for leaving coaching, but you saw something in me that others didn't.

Molly Crippen, for teaching me **so much** about

leadership and how to bring the best out of people. Thank you for your decades-long friendship.

Ron Rosbruch, for proving that nice guys can finish first. You have built a remarkable organization with class and dignity.

My Wealth Design Group family, for helping me accomplish my goals and for the wonderful times we have shared together. We have accomplished so much and I know the best is yet to come.

My fellow Guardian General Agents for the example you have set for me over the years. You truly are "best in class," and I admire you.

My writer, Stephen Palmer, for helping me get my thoughts and beliefs onto paper.

Last but certainly not least, God, for providing me with the wisdom in Probers 16:3 many years ago: "Entrust your work to the Lord, and your planning will succeed."

NOTES

Introduction

1. The story of Matt Weinstein was relayed by Matt himself to a friend of mine, Steve D'Annunzio.
2. Wikipedia, http://en.wikipedia.org/wiki/Bernard_Madoff
3. "How Bernie Did It," CNN Money, April 30, 2009, http://money.cnn.com/2009/04/24/news/newsmakers/madoff.fortune/
4. "The Bernie Madoff Client List is Made Public," Time Magazine, February 5, 2009, http://content.time.com/time/business/article/0,8599,1877414,00.html
5. http://www.evansfinancialgroup.com/Term_lifeInsurance.html

Chapter 2

6. Krom, Erik, "Solving the Myth of Rate of Return," April 30, 2012 http://www.foxbusiness.com/personal-finance/2012/04/30/solving-myth-rate-return/

   Dow Jones Industrial Average is a widely used indicator of the overall condition of the stock market, a price-weighted average of 30 actively traded blue chip stocks, primarily industrials. Past performance is not a guarantee of future results. Indices are unmanaged and one cannot invest directly in an index.

7. https://eyfpc.com/LinkClick.aspx?fileticket=bNMX3hLANh8%3D&tabid=234&mid=584&language=en-US

Chapter 4

8. http://youtu.be/9NeSpPgmYQc

USEFUL RESOURCES

Wealth Design Group
wealthdesigngroup.net

Social Security
ssa.gov

National Debt Clock
usdebtclock.org

Living Balance Sheet
livingbalancesheet.com

Mortgage Calculator
mortgagecalculator.org

IRS
irs.gov

Tax Calendar for Business and Self-Employed
tax.gov/calendar/

FINRA
finra.org

SEC
sec.gov

Matson Money
matsonmoney.com

A.M. Best Company
ambest.com

Asset Protection
assetprotectionbook.com

Retirement Planning
tomhegna.com

Retirement Statistics
statisticbrain.com/retirement-statistics/

Financial Balance
Youtube.com (search financial balance)

Top 10 Retirement Risks
marketwatch.com/story/ten-major-retirement-risks-tips

A Few Great Books

Paychecks and Playchecks by Tom Hegna

How to Run Your Business So You Can Leave in Style by John Brown

Main Street Money by Mark Matson

The Little Book of Behavioral Investing by James Montier

The Prosperity Paradigm by Steve D'Annunzio

Your Complete Retirement Road Map by Ed Slott

Responsible Wealth by Frank Congilose

Secrets of the Millionaire Mind by Harv Eker

The Millionaire Next Door by Thomas Stanley and William Danko

The Richest Man in Babylon by George Clason

Killing Sacred Cows by Garret Gunderson

The Creature from Jekyll Island by Edward Griffin

The Pirates of Manhattan by Barry James Dyke

Confessions of a CPA by Bryan Bloom